WORDS
YOU SHOULD KNOW
HOW TO SPELL

WORDS
YOU SHOULD KNOW
HOW TO SPELL

AN A TO Z GUIDE TO PERFECT SPELLING

David Hatcher, MA and Jane Mallison, MA

Avon, Massachusetts

Published by
Adams Media, a division of F+W Media, Inc.
57 Littlefield Street, Avon, MA 02322. U.S.A.
www.adamsmedia.com

ISBN 10: 1-4405-0616-7
ISBN 13: 978-1-4405-0616-1
eISBN 10: 1-4405-0733-3
eISBN 13: 978-1-4405-0733-5

Printed in the United States of America.

10 9 8 7 6 5 4 3 2 1

Library of Congress Cataloging-in-Publication Data
is available from the publisher.

This publication is designed to provide accurate and authoritative information
with regard to the subject matter covered. It is sold with the understanding
that the publisher is not engaged in rendering legal, accounting, or other
professional advice. If legal advice or other expert assistance is required, the
services of a competent professional person should be sought.

—From a *Declaration of Principles* jointly adopted by a
Committee of the American Bar Association and a
Committee of Publishers and Associations

Many of the designations used by manufacturers and sellers to distinguish
their product are claimed as trademarks. Where those designations appear
in this book and Adams Media was aware of a trademark claim, the
designations have been printed with initial capital letters.

This book is available at quantity discounts for bulk purchases.
For information, please call 1-800-289-0963.

To John Pitman, our journalism
teacher, who taught us to
choose our words with care.

Acknowledgments

We both extend our deep appreciation to Lane
Goddard, whose skills—with language and software—
and untiring efforts were so valuable.

We also want to thank our most-careful editors—
Lisa Laing, Elizabeth Kassab, and Katie Corcoran Lytle—
and special thanks to our ever-helpful agent, Grace
Freedson.

grammasion privele
rouse hexagonnal sa
cheeve trajectory ma
xtract grimey readi

Introduction

"I put a spell on you / Because you're mine." Whether sung languorously by Nina Simone or wildly by Screamin' Jay Hawkins, these lines from the song "I Put a Spell on You" remind us of a peculiar truth. The noun "spell" with its meaning of a charm put on someone stems from the very same word as "spell," the verb that refers to naming off the letters that make up a word.

This surprising ancestry lets us start off this introduction to *Words You Should Know How to Spell* with a more glamorous aura than spelling usually receives. Equally startling is the fact that the word "glamor" is a variant of the word "grammar." Those of us with awful memories of underlining the subject once and the verb twice find it amazing—but it's essentially the same story. Having power over words was what seemingly gave sorcerers their prowess. In a world where recording devices lay far in the future and where most people were illiterate, the very phenomenon of writing packed a magic of its own. Imagine being able to preserve a thought forever by making some little scratch marks! Today, writing is not as novel; nonetheless, power over words remains a vitally important skill.

WHY IS SPELLING IMPORTANT?

A misspelled word in an otherwise well-executed report is like egg on the face of an otherwise impeccably turned-out individual. At a minimum, misspellings can suggest sloppiness, a telling lack of attention to detail. No one wants to write "You are my best fried" to his buddy, although, of course, the buddy will know what you mean. Yes, good friends do read our minds, but we can't count on mental telepathy with everyone. At their worst, misspellings can lead to downright confusion and misinterpretation. If you received an e-mail that said a co-worker had a "rye look" on his face, you might think of meanings that a "wry look" could never convey. Similarly, an imminent storm has only a minuscule chance of becoming an eminent storm. (And yes, "minuscule" is related to the world of math— "minus"—not to the world of tiny—"mini.")

WHY DO WE MISSPELL?

What's the source of spelling errors? Carelessness, for starters. Lack of sufficient knowledge. Textual editors of F. Scott Fitzgerald, a notoriously weak speller, are still wondering about Fitzgerald's use of "orgastic" near the end of *The Great Gatsby*. Did he mean "orgiastic?" "Orgasmic?" We don't know. Sometimes, particularly in informal contexts, spelling variants are intentional. They can signal proud rebellion against the mainstream as in the spelling of "boys" in the movie *Boyz n the Hood*. Using a *z* instead of an *s* for a plural has gained some currency. Will it ever lose its rebel status and infiltrate mainstream spelling? It's possible—the plural of "eye" used to be "eyne"—but none of us are likely to be around for the corporate report that refers to stockz and bondz.

Similarly, technological developments that began in the late twentieth century have made most people—particularly those under, say, thirty—users of a new kind of spelling shorthand. R U OK? Gr8! C U at 9. (*New Yorker* writer Adam Gopnik had a wonderful anecdote about frequent instant messaging with his teenage son—who was in the next room—and believing for months that his son's "LOL" sign-off meant "lots of love.") Expressions like these make you an instant member of an in-group, but their primary benefit is speed. You want to be quick about answering your pal—especially if you're typing with your thumb. Will any of these abbreviations ever come into standard English? The letter and number hybrid has a certain chirpy appeal, but it would seem inappropriate to read that the patient was "4tunate that the lab test showed the 2mor 2B B9." Police dogs as members of the K-9 corps may be as far as this device will go, but you never know—historians of the early days of printing inform us that some spellings were altered because printers needed more or fewer letters to justify their margins.

Yes, many factors produce deviations from orthodox spelling. Perhaps foremost among them is the very nature of the English language. Writers of Italian and Spanish—those beautifully phonetic tongues—need to worry much less about spelling; it's the spelling of English that is inconsistent, irregular, and (some say) insane. Mark Twain is well known for a hilarious piece called "The Awful German Language," but he might have done an equally elaborate onslaught on English, a language that once spelled ghost "gost" (which replicates its sound) but went to "ghost," the Dutch spelling, under the influence of one individual. Other wits and linguists have made the public aware of how thorny English spelling is. (Consider the pronunciation of the similarly spelled "rough," "cough," and "through," and rejoice that the western hemisphere has dropped the British "plough" and "hiccough.")

COULDN'T SPELLING BE SIMPLER?

Over the centuries, language experts and laypeople have advocated reform. Perhaps most famous to ordinary users of the language is George Bernard Shaw, who left money in his will to reward the creator of the best phonetic (fonetik?) alphabet in English. (The winner and his system were soon forgotten.) Similarly, it was Shaw who called our attention to the fact that "ghoti" could be a logical spelling for "fish": *gh* as in "cough," *o* as in "women," and *ti* as in "nation." Even Theodore Roosevelt weighed in on the subject of spelling, with a plea that our spelling be made "a little less foolish and fantastic."

Despite this off-and-on hubbub, nothing much has changed. Yes, in the United States we can now write "humor," not "humour," but we're still writing "thorough" for what sounds like "thuro." Not to mention that we write (or try to write) "ophthalmology" for a word almost everyone pronounces "ofthamology." If you decide to work for—or at least to cheer for—further radical changes in standard English spelling, fine. In the meantime, you're going to have to cope with the current system as best you can.

WHAT ABOUT SPELL CHECK?

We're not mind readers, but we suspect you've been thinking, "but spell check has changed all that!" To some extent, yes—and hurrah for that! But as many writers have learned the hard way, spellcheckers can sometimes hurt. Have you ever offered spell check a misspelling and gotten back something far from what you had in mind? A friend was recently trying to write "nonchalant." Spell check's best guess was "non-sealant"—not quite the same thing! Similarly, the spell check program of an acquaintance in the health profession let him down badly when a draft of a report referred to chronic *hick upping*. Even worse, spelling checkers are totally impotent in regard to determining what correctly spelled word fits your context. When you write that the vice president of the company had "free reign" to make decisions, your spell checker doesn't know that you meant to use "free rein," a metaphor drawn not from royalty but from horses. And although many people have their laptops practically welded to their hands, some of us still have moments of writing when we're away from a computer and its program.

YOU CAN BE A BETTER SPELLER

It's not only helpful to bulk up the spelling lobe of your brain; it's also possible. This book can help you. Let's begin to look at some specifics. As you glance through this book, you'll see columns of common misspellings and their correct counterparts. You now have instant access to the correct spelling of more than 12,500 words, organized with speed and convenience in mind. This book takes the guesswork out of spelling. In our Spell It Right Appendix you'll also find various cautions, memory hooks, notes about words that do or do not follow rules, and guides to help you sort out tricky pairs such as *affect* and *effect* or triplets like *censor*, *sensor*, and *censure*. Adopting our tips and memory tricks can assist you, and beginning to work out tips and hooks of your own can be even more beneficial. This dictionary also helps by being a book that fits in your hand, your pocket, and your bag. Whatever your goal, this is the book for you!

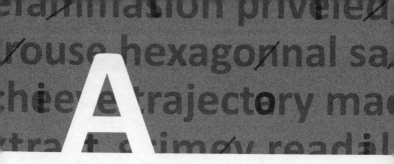

Most Commonly Misspelled Words

- absence
- accommodate
- achieve
- acquire
- address
- among
- apparent
- argument
- athlete
- awful

Incorrect	Correct	Incorrect	Correct
a capella	a cappella	abbscond	abscond
a pryori	a priori	abbsentee	absentee
abac	aback	abbsolution	absolution
abait	abate	abbsolve	absolve
abasse	abase	abbstemious	abstemious
abayence	abeyance	abbstruse	abstruse
abba	abbé	abbusive	abusive
abbacus	abacus	abbutment	abutment
abbaft	abaft	abby	abbé
abbalishionist	abolitionist	abbye	abbey
abbaloney	abalone	abbysmal	abysmal
abbandon	abandon	abbzorption	absorption
abbariginal	aboriginal	abdacate	abdicate
abbash	abash	abdommen	abdomen
abbatement	abatement	abdomminal	abdominal
abbatoire	abattoir	Abell	Abel
abbcissa	abscissa	abeyence	abeyance
abbduct	abduct	abhore	abhor
abbduction	abduction	abhorent	abhorrent
abberation	aberration	abhorrance	abhorrence
abberent	aberrant	abiss	abyss
abbet	abet	abissal	abyssal
abblative	ablative	abjoor	abjure
abblaze	ablaze	abnagate	abnegate
abbolish	abolish	abnagation	abnegation
abbolition	abolition	abnormallity	abnormality
abbominable	abominable	aborshun	abortion
abboriginee	aborigine	abrevviate	abbreviate
abbott	abbot	abscent	absent
abbracadabra	abracadabra	absense	absence
abbrasive	abrasive	abserd	absurd
abbrazzo	abrazo	absess	abscess
abbrupt	abrupt	absorbant	absorbent
abbs	abs	abstension	abstention

Incorrect	Correct	Incorrect	Correct
abstinance	abstinence	accordian	accordion
abundence	abundance	accresion	accretion
abundent	abundant	accrid	acrid
abzurdity	absurdity	accrobat	acrobat
acadamy	academy	accronym	acronym
acanthis	acanthus	accrophobia	acrophobia
acauaintence	acquaintance	accropolis	acropolis
accacia	acacia	accros	across
accademia	academia	accrostic	acrostic
accanthus	acanthus	accruel	accrual
accarage	acreage	acction	action
acceed	accede	acctress	actress
accelaration	acceleration	accuantance	acquaintance
accellerator	accelerator	accuity	acuity
accellerent	accelerant	acculzition	acquisition
accensuate	accentuate	accummulate	accumulate
acceptible	acceptable	accupuncture	acupuncture
accesable	accessible	accurracy	accuracy
accesory	accessory	accurrsed	accursed
accetic	acetic	accusitive	accusative
accidense	accidence	accustic	acoustic
accidic	acidic	accustum	accustom
accidintly	accidentally	accute	acute
acclame	acclaim	accuzation	accusation
acclammation	acclamation	accuze	accuse
acclimmate	acclimate	accuzing	accusing
accollade	accolade	acentuate	accentuate
accolyte	acolyte	acerbait	acerbate
accomodate	accommodate	acettaline	acetylene
acccompanniment	accompaniment	acheeve	achieve
accompleshmant	accomplishment	achevement	achievement
accomplise	accomplice	achey	achy
accooter	accouter	achrommatic	achromatic
accordence	accordance	aciditty	acidity

Incorrect	Correct	Incorrect	Correct
acidoffalous	acidophilus	actionible	actionable
acke	ache	activaties	activities
Ackeron	Acheron	actuallity	actuality
Ackilles heel	Achilles heel	actualy	actually
ackmee	acme	acturrial	actuarial
acknollege	acknowledge	actuwary	actuary
ackny	acne	aculturate	acculturate
ackorn	acorn	add hock	ad hoc
ackrylic	acrylic	add homanem	ad hominem
ackseed	accede	add infinitem	ad infinitum
acksent	accent	add lib	ad lib
acksess	access	add nauseum	ad nauseam
ackwire	acquire	add vallorem	ad valorem
ackwit	acquit	addage	adage
aclat	eclat	addamantine	adamantine
acomplish	accomplish	addapt	adapt
acost	accost	addaquit	adequate
acountant	accountant	addative	additive
acouterment	accouterment	addeau	adieu
acqueus	aqueous	addel	addle
acquiese	acquiesce	addendam	addendum
acquiesence	acquiescence	addenoyds	adenoids
acquisative	acquisitive	addept	adept
acquital	acquittal	addhere	adhere
acquited	acquitted	addherent	adherent
acredit	accredit	addhezive	adhesive
acrillic	acrylic	addic	addict
acrimoneus	acrimonious	addipose	adipose
acromeggaly	acromegaly	addit	adit
acsellarate	accelerate	addjative	adjective
acsept	accept	addjudge	adjudge
actavate	activate	addjunk	adjunct
actavism	activism	addjutent	adjutant
acter	actor	addmit	admit

A

Incorrect	Correct	Incorrect	Correct
addmonision	admonition	adrennal	adrenal
addobe	adobe	adress	address
addopt	adopt	adroyte	adroit
addore	adore	adsorbant	adsorbent
addorn	adorn	adultary	adultery
adduccion	adduction	adulterrate	adulterate
addulate	adulate	adulterrer	adulterer
adduse	adduce	adulterrous	adulterous
addvantage	advantage	adverbeal	adverbial
addvantageous	advantageous	adversaty	adversity
addventuress	adventuress	advisary	advisory
addverse	adverse	advizable	advisable
addvertlze	advertise	advizement	advisement
addze	adz	advocasy	advocacy
addze	adze	advoccate	advocate
adelvise	edelweiss	Aeolean	Aeolian
ademant	adamant	afect	affect (change)
adherance	adherence	affadavit	affidavit
adhezion	adhesion	affar	afar
adjoor	adjure	affebel	affable
adjurn	adjourn	affeck	affect
admier	admire	affectasion	affectation
administrater	administrator	afficiannodo	aficionado
adminnister	administer	affid	aphid
admirasion	admiration	afflame	aflame
admirrel	admiral	afflic	afflict
admittence	admittance	afflicksion	affliction
admonnish	admonish	afflote	afloat
adollescence	adolescence	affluense	affluence
adollescent	adolescent	afflutter	aflutter
Adonnis	Adonis	affoot	afoot
adoo	ado	afforist	aphorist
adorrable	adorable	affresh	afresh
Adreatic	Adriatic	Affro	Afro

Incorrect	Correct	Incorrect	Correct
affter	after	aggree	agree
affterberth	afterbirth	aggreed	agreed
afftermath	aftermath	aggrement	agreement
affterward	afterward	aggresser	aggressor
affterword	afterword	aggriculture	agriculture
afilliate	affiliate	aggronemy	agronomy
afilliated	affiliated	aggue	ague
afilliation	affiliation	agid	aged
afinnity	affinity	agism	ageism
afirm	affirm	agonise	agonize
afirmattive	affirmative	agorra	agora
afix	affix	agrabusiness	agribusiness
afluent	affluent	agreeible	agreeable
aformentioned	aforementioned	agressive	aggressive
afray	affray	agrumentattive	argumentative
afrodisiac	aphrodisiac	ahhoy	ahoy
Afrokans	Afrikaans	ahn garde	en garde
afront	affront	ahnt	aunt
agap	agape	ahnvoy	envoy
agarric	agaric	aidd	aid (help)
aggain	again	aidd	aide (helper)
aggar-aggar	agar-agar	AIDDS	AIDS (disease)
aggate	agate	aigth	eighth
aggency	agency	ailleron	aileron
aggent provoccateur	agent provocateur	ailllurephile	ailurophile
aggervate	aggravate	airabble	arable
aggitater	agitator	airborn	airborne
aggonize	agonize	Airdale	Airedale
aggony	agony	airloom	heirloom
aggorophobia	agoraphobia	airobattics	aerobatics
aggove	agave	airomechanics	aeromechanics
aggranomics	agronomics	aironaut	aeronaut
aggraphia	agraphia	aironautical	aeronautical
aggrarian	agrarian	aironautics	aeronautics

Incorrect	Correct	Incorrect	Correct
airosol	aerosol	alfoulfa	alfalfa
airospace	aerospace	algee	algae (plural)
airplain	airplane	algi	alga (singular)
airr	heir (inheritor)	algorythm	algorithm
aite	eight	alian	alien
aiy-aiy	aye-aye	alianthus	ailanthus
ajile	agile	alkahaul	alcohol
ajility	agility	alkahollic	alcoholic
ajinda	agenda	alkalie	alkali
ajjar	ajar	alkalloid	alkaloid
ajoin	adjoin	alkammy	alchemy
ajudicate	adjudicate	Alkatrazz	Alcatraz
akkimbo	akimbo	alkilyze	alkalize
akkin	akin	alla cart	a la carte
akute	acute	alla mode	a la mode
al denty	al dente		(stylish, or with ice cream)
Al Kaidda	al Qaeda	alla mode	alamode
alagory	allegory		(silk fabric)
alass	alas	allabaster	alabaster
alay	allay	allaby	alibi
Albakerky	Albuquerque	allacate	allocate
albanism	albinism	allagation	allegation
albe	alb	allagator	alligator
albuman	albumin	allagorical	allegorical
alchaemy	alchemy	allamode	alamode (silk)
aleanate	alienate	allamonde	allemande
alegiance	allegiance	allamony	alimony
alegretto	allegretto	allaphone	allophone
alegro	allegro	allbacore	albacore
Aleuit	Aleut	allbatross	albatross
aleviate	alleviate	allbeit	albeit
Alexandrea	Alexandria	allbum	album
alfa and ommega	alpha and omega	allderman	alderman
alfanumerric	alphanumeric	alleas	alias

Incorrect	Correct	Incorrect	Correct
alledge	allege	allreddy	all ready (prepared)
allee	alee		
allembic	alembic	alltar	altar (stand)
allergee	allergy	allter	alter (change)
allert	alert	allterasion	alteration
Alleut	Aleut	alltercation	altercation
Alleutian	Aleutian	allternative	alternative
allexia	alexia	allternator	alternator
allfa	alpha	allthough	although
allfresco	alfresco	alltogather	altogether (completely)
allgebra	algebra		
allie	alley (passageway)	alltogether	all together (combined)
allie	ally (friend)	allum	alum
allience	alliance	allumnas	alumnus
allight	alight	allvaolur	alveolar
allike	alike	allways	always
alline	align	ally-oop	alley-oop
allit	alit	Allzhiemer's disease	Alzheimer's disease
allitarasion	alliteration		
allmanack	almanac	alma matter	alma mater
allmighty	almighty	alot	allot (give)
allmond	almond	alot	a lot (many)
allmost	almost	alow	allow
allms	alms	alowance	allowance
alloe	aloe	alowed	allowed (permitted)
alloft	aloft		
allone	alone	aloy	alloy
alloof	aloof	alpacka	alpaca
allopecia	alopecia	alphorne	alphorn
alloted	allotted	alreddy	all ready (prepared)
alloud	aloud (heard)		
Allpine	Alpine	alreddy	already (past)
allready	already (past)	alright	all right

Incorrect	Correct	Incorrect	Correct
altatude	altitude	ammid	amid
altimmeter	altimeter	ammidships	amidships
altocumulous	altocumulus	ammigdala	amygdala
altrueism	altruism	ammiss	amiss
altruistick	altruistic	ammneosentesis	amniocentesis
alude	allude (refer)	ammorous	amorous
aluminnium	aluminum	ammorphus	amorphous
alure	allure	ammortazation	amortization
alussion	allusion	ammortise	amortize
aluvial	alluvial	ammount	amount
amalgum	amalgam	ammour	amour
amalgumate	amalgamate	ammpersand	ampersand
amannuensis	amanuensis	ammpitheater	amphitheater
amature	amateur	ammuk	amok
ambadexterous	ambidextrous	ammung	among
ambaguety	ambiguity	ammuze	amuse
ambeant	ambient	amnezia	amnesia
ambeyance	ambience	amnisty	amnesty
ambigguous	ambiguous	amonnia	ammonia
ambivulant	ambivalent	amorral	amoral
ambullence	ambulance	ampeer	ampere
ameeba	amoeba	amperrage	amperage
amfora	amphora	amphettamine	amphetamine
ammandine	amandine	amphibbean	amphibian
ammathyst	amethyst	amphibbious	amphibious
ammative	amative	ampile	ample
ammber	amber	amplafy	amplify
ammego	amigo	amplatude	amplitude
ammenable	amenable	ampull	ampoule
ammenity	amenity	amputtee	amputee
ammeno	amino	amulett	amulet
ammenorea	amenorrhea	amunition	ammunition
ammentia	amentia	amyable	amiable
ammicable	amicable	anafrodisiac	anaphrodisiac

Incorrect	Correct	Incorrect	Correct
analyasis	analysis	animuss	animus
anarky	anarchy	anisthetic	anesthetic
Anartick	Antarctic	anjina	angina
anceint	ancient	anjioplasty	angioplasty
ancestrel	ancestral	anker	anchor
anchorege	anchorage	ankorage	anchorage
anchorrite	anchorite	anklette	anklet
anclave	enclave	Annababtist	Anabaptist
ancore	encore	annachronism	anachronism
andirron	andiron	annaconda	anaconda
andontay	andante	annagram	anagram
andragen	androgen	annal	anal
androjenous	androgynous	annalgesic	analgesic
Andrommeda	Andromeda	annalize	analyze
androyd	android	annalls	annals
aneal	anneal	annalog	analog
anel	anal	annalogy	analogy
anemmanee	anemone	annalyst	analyst
anex	annex	annalytic	analytic
angellic	angelic	annamometer	anemometer
angest	angst	annanimmity	anonymity
Anglacism	Anglicism	annapest	anapest
Anglo Saxxon	Anglo Saxon	annarchist	anarchist
Anglofile	Anglophile	annarobic	anaerobic
angorra	angora	annatate	annotate
angryer	angrier	annathema	anathema
angryest	angriest	annatomy	anatomy
angstrum	angstrom	annchovy	anchovy
angul	angle	annecdotal	anecdotal
anguler	angular	annecdote	anecdote
angziety	anxiety	annellid	annelid
animacule	animalcule	annemia	anemia
animasm	animism	anngler	angler
animossity	animosity	annguish	anguish

Incorrect	Correct	Incorrect	Correct
annihillate	annihilate	antagonnizm	antagonism
annimadversion	animadversion	antalope	antelope
annimate	animate	antamatter	antimatter
annimation	animation	antapasto	antipasto
annise	anise (flower, seed)	Antartick	Antarctic
		antaseptic	antiseptic
annisette	anisette (liqueur)	ante merridium	ante meridiem
anniversery	anniversary	antecedant	antecedent
annode	anode	antechrist	antichrist
annoey	annoy	antecoagulent	anticoagulant
annorexic	anorexic	antedilluvean	antediluvian
annorexxia	anorexia	anteek	antique
annoyence	annoyance	antemony	antimony
annser	answer	anthollogy	anthology
annterior	anterior	anthrasite	anthracite
annthem	anthem	anthropoffagi	anthropophagi
annthrax	anthrax	anthropollogy	anthropology
annuel	annual	anthroposentric	anthropocentric
annuitee	annuity	anthroppoid	anthropoid
annuitent	annuitant	antibacterrial	antibacterial
annurism	aneurysm	antibalistic	antiballistic
annus	anus	anticippate	anticipate
annvil	anvil	antick	antic
anomallous	anomalous	antidate	antedate
anomally	anomaly	antideppressent	antidepressant
anonnamous	anonymous	antidissestablishmentareanism	
anoynt	anoint		antidisestablishmentarianism
ansestor	ancestor	antidoat	antidote
ansillery	ancillary	antihistammine	antihistamine
antabiotic	antibiotic	anti-intellectuel	anti-intellectual
antaboddy	antibody	antimacasser	antimacassar
antacyclone	anticyclone	antinna	antenna
antagen	antigen	antinym	antonym
antaggonize	antagonize	antioxident	antioxidant

Incorrect	Correct	Incorrect	Correct
antipathey	antipathy	aportion	apportion
antipenultimmate	antepenultimate	apositive	appositive
antipersonal	antipersonnel	apothecarry	apothecary
antiperspirrant	antiperspirant	appace	apace
antipodez	antipodes	appal	appall
antiquarean	antiquarian	Appalachean	Appalachian
antiqwated	antiquated	appaplexy	apoplexy
antisemmitic	anti-Semitic	apparant	apparent
antissipitory	anticipatory	apparatchick	apparatchik
antithessis	antithesis	apparattus	apparatus
antitoxxin	antitoxin	apparision	apparition
antivennin	antivenin	apparrel	apparel
antivivvisection	antivivisection	appathy	apathy
antraprenure	entrepreneur	appatite	appetite
antybellum	antebellum	appawl	appall
anuelly	annually	appearence	appearance
anull	annul	appelasion	appellation
anullment	annulment	appellent	appellant
anxius	anxious	appendaces	appendices
aoarta	aorta	appendacitis	appendicitis
Aolein	Aeolian	appendectamy	appendectomy
apalled	appalled	appendege	appendage
apalling	appalling	appetising	appetizing
apaloosa	appaloosa	appiary	apiary
apay	epee	appiece	apiece
apeal	appeal	appithet	epithet
apear	appear	applacant	applicant
apease	appease	applacation	application
apendix	appendix	applaque	appliqué
aperature	aperture	applaude	applaud
aperteef	aperitif	applaus	applause
aphrodiziac	aphrodisiac	applenty	aplenty
apiarry	apiary	applicabel	applicable
apocryphel	apocryphal	applience	appliance

Incorrect	Correct	Incorrect	Correct
appocalypse	apocalypse	aquattic	aquatic
appogee	apogee	auqculture	aquaculture
appologize	apologize	aquilline	aquiline
appoplectic	apoplectic	arabesk	arabesque
appostacy	apostasy	arain	arraign
appostel	apostle	arass	arras
appostrophe	apostrophe	Arayan	Aryan
appothem	apothegm	arbatrage	arbitrage
appotheosis	apotheosis	arbatrary	arbitrary
appozible	opposable	arbatrate	arbitrate
apprahend	apprehend	arbatration	arbitration
apprapo	apropos	arbitter	arbiter
appreceate	appreciate	arbor vita	arborvitae
appricot	apricot	arborretum	arboretum
appron	apron	arborrial	arboreal
appropreate	appropriate	arbur	arbor
appse	apse	arbutas	arbutus
appurtnence	appurtenance	arcaid	arcade
apraise	appraise	archary	archery
aprehension	apprehension	archdiosese	archdiocese
aprentice	apprentice	arche	arch
aprise	apprise	archenamy	archenemy
aproach	approach	Archimeades	Archimedes
aproval	approval	archipelligo	archipelago
aprove	approve	architec	architect
aproximate	approximate	architecter	architecture
aptarix	apteryx	archyopteryx	archaeopteryx
aptittude	aptitude	ardant	ardent
aqqua	aqua	arder	ardor
aqua vitea	aqua vitae	ardous	arduous
aquaduct	aqueduct	ardvark	aardvark
aquafur	aquifer	areal	aerial
aquaint	acquaint	arears	arrears
aquaream	aquarium	areate	aerate

Incorrect	Correct	Incorrect	Correct
areater	aerator	arrahead	arrowhead
arest	arrest	Arramaic	Aramaic
Argentena	Argentina	arrangemant	arrangement
argossy	argosy	arranje	arrange
argueable	arguable	Ararat	Ararat
arguemint	argument	arraroot	arrowroot
arguile	argyle	arrayel	arrayal
argut	argot	arree	aerie
argyoo	argue	arrena	arena
arial	aerial	arrent	arrant
aristocrasy	aristocracy	arreola	areola
arithmatick	arithmetic	arrgon	argon
arithmeticlky	arithmetically	arrgyle	argyle
arkaic	archaic	arrhythmea	arrhythmia
arkane	arcane	arria	aria
arkangel	archangel	arrid	arid
arke	ark (boat, box)	arright	aright
arke	arc (curve)	arrise	arise
arkeology	archaeology	aristocrat	aristocrat
arketype	archetype	arrivaderche	arrivederci
arkives	archives	arrmada	armada
Armagedden	Armageddon	arrogel	aerogel
armamant	armament	arroma	aroma
armary	armory	arromatic	aromatic
armastice	armistice	arround	around
armeture	armature	arrouse	arouse
armidillo	armadillo	arrugula	arugula
armoir	armoire	arrum	arum
arogance	arrogance	arsanic	arsenic
arpaggio	arpeggio	arsannel	arsenal
arrabesque	arabesque	arsson	arson
arrachnid	arachnid	art decko	art deco
arrachnoid	arachnoid	artachoke	artichoke
arragant	arrogant	artafact	artifact

Incorrect	Correct	Incorrect	Correct
artafice	artifice	asist	assist
artaficial	artificial	askanse	askance
artarry	artery	asociate	associate
artereal	arterial	asort	assort
artezean	artesian	aspan	aspen
arthrapod	arthropod	asparragus	asparagus
arthritick	arthritic	aspe	asp
arthritus	arthritis	asperation	aspiration
artic	arctic	asperraty	asperity
articullate	articulate	aspirent	aspirant
articullation	articulation	asprine	aspirin
artifacs	artifacts	assale	assail
artillary	artillery	assanine	asinine
artizan	artisan	assasin	assassin
asault	assault	assatone	acetone
asay	assay	asscot	ascot
asbestus	asbestos	asscribe	ascribe
ascendint	ascendent	asseffalus	acephalous
ascention	ascension	assembledge	assemblage
ascettic	ascetic	assemmbly	assembly
asent	assent	assend	ascend
aseptick	aseptic	asserbaty	acerbity
asert	assert	asserbic	acerbic
asess	assess	assersion	assertion
asetts	assets	assertain	ascertain
asexuel	asexual	assesser	assessor
asfault	asphalt	assetaline	acetylene
asfixiate	asphyxiate	assett	asset
ashan	ashen	asseverrate	asseverate
ashrem	ashram	Assian	Asian
asignation	assignation	Assiatic	Asiatic
asilum	asylum	assidous	assiduous
asimmilate	assimilate	assimetrical	asymmetrical
asimtottick	asymptotic	assine	assign

Incorrect	Correct	Incorrect	Correct
assininaty	asininity	atarr	attar
Assissi	Assisi	ateen	eighteen
assistence	assistance	atenuate	attenuate
assonence	assonance	atest	attest
assoom	assume	athalete	athlete
asspect	aspect	athalettic	athletic
asspersion	aspersion	atheizm	atheism
asspire	aspire	atherosclarossis	atherosclerosis
assthma	asthma	atinngle	atingle
asstound	astound	atire	attire
asstringent	astringent	Atlantick	Atlantic
assumpsion	assumption	Atlantiss	Atlantis
assunder	asunder	atmasphere	atmosphere
assurence	assurance	atoufay	étouffée
asta luego	hasta luego	atracity	atrocity
astaroid	asteroid	atreum	atrium
astericks	asterisk	atribute	attribute
astigmatizm	astigmatism	attachay	attaché
astonnish	astonish	attachmant	attachment
astoot	astute	attander	attainder
astor	aster	attane	attain
astradome	astrodome	attatude	attitude
astranaut	astronaut	attavism	atavism
astranautical	astronautical	attellea	atelier
astraphysics	astrophysics	attemp	attempt
Astraturf	Astroturf	attendence	attendance
astrollogy	astrology	attension	attention
astronommical	astronomical	attick	attic
asturn	astern	attol	atoll
asuage	assuage	attomic	atomic
asurb	acerb	attomize	atomize
asymetry	asymmetry	attonal	atonal
atach	attach	attop	atop
atack	attack	attornies	attorneys

Incorrect	Correct	Incorrect	Correct
attrabute	attribute	auspisces	auspices
attracsion	attraction	auspiscious	auspicious
attribusion	attribution	austeer	austere
attrision	attrition	Australlia	Australia
attrocious	atrocious	autem	autumn
attrofie	atrophy	autharitarian	authoritarian
attunne	attune	autharize	authorize
au contrare	au contraire	autharizing	authorizing
au gratten	au gratin	authentick	authentic
au naturrele	au naturel	authoritattive	authoritative
aucsion	auction	authur	author
aucsioneer	auctioneer	autobiografy	autobiography
audable	audible	Autobonn	Autobahn
audaccious	audacious	autocrasy	autocracy
audassity	audacity	autocratt	autocrat
audiance	audience	autodidac	autodidact
audiollogy	audiology	autoerrotic	autoerotic
audiovizual	audiovisual	autograff	autograph
auditoreum	auditorium	autohipnosis	autohypnosis
auditt	audit	autoimune	autoimmune
audittion	audition	automattion	automation
audittor	auditor	automatton	automaton
Audobon	Audubon	autonnomous	autonomous
auer	hour	autonnomy	autonomy
augary	augury	autonommic	autonomic
auggar	auger (tool)	autoppsy	autopsy
augger	augur	autorchy	autarchy
aughte	aught	auttoharp	autoharp
augmint	augment	autumnel	autumnal
Augusst	August	autysm	autism
aul	awl	auxillery	auxiliary
aurra	aura	avacado	avocado
aurrora borealis	aurora borealis	avale	avail
Auschwits	Auschwitz	averiss	avarice

Incorrect	Correct	Incorrect	Correct
averzion	aversion	awburn	auburn
avoidence	avoidance	awefully	awfully
avont-guard	avant-garde	awfull	awful
avordapoi	avoirdupois	awk	auk
avouche	avouch	awkwerd	awkward
avunculler	avuncular	awrie	awry
avvalanche	avalanche	awwe	awe
avvatar	avatar	awweigh	aweigh
avvenge	avenge	axiommatic	axiomatic
avvenue	avenue	axxe	axe
avver	aver	axxel	axle
avverage	average	axxiom	axiom
avverse	averse	axxis	axis
avvert	avert	ayatolla	ayatollah
avvian	avian	aysle	aisle
avviation	aviation	Ayurvedda	Ayurveda
avviatrix	aviatrix	azalia	azalea
avvid	avid	azmuh	asthma
avvocation	avocation	azzimuth	azimuth
avvoid	avoid	Azztec	Aztec
awakenning	awakening	azzure	azure

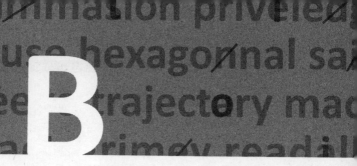

Most Commonly Misspelled Words

- baffle
- balance
- balloon
- beginning
- believe
- benefit
- beverage
- bicycle
- breathe
- business

Incorrect	Correct	Incorrect	Correct
baba oh room	baba au rhum	baizh	beige
Babbalon	Babylon	balefull	baleful
babbel	babble	balene	baleen
Babbit	Babbitt	baleywick	bailiwick
babboon	baboon	balisstic	ballistic
babbushka	babushka	ball pean	ball peen
Babell	Babel	ballalika	balalaika
Babtist	Baptist	ballance	balance
babtize	baptize	ballarena	ballerina
baccalarette	baccalaureate	ballay	ballet
baccarrat	baccarat	balletamane	balletomane
baccon	bacon	ballistrade	balustrade
Bachous	Bacchus	ballitt	ballot
backannal	bacchanal	ballodd	ballad
backgamon	backgammon	ballony	bologna
backho	backhoe	ballsa	balsa
backwatter	backwater	ballsum	balsam
bacterria	bacteria	Balltic	Baltic
badinaze	badinage	ballust	ballast
badje	badge	balmey	balmy
badjer	badger	baloon	balloon
badminten	badminton	bambinno	bambino
baeth	bathe (verb)	bamboozzle	bamboozle
baffel	baffle	bammboo	bamboo
Baggdad	Baghdad	bandaleer	bandoleer
baggaje	baggage	bandidge	bandage
baggatele	bagatelle	bandycoot	bandicoot
baggel	bagel	Bangaloor	Bangalore
baggette	baguette	bankrupp	bankrupt
Baha California	Baja California	bankruppsy	bankruptcy
Bahammas	Bahamas	bannal	banal
bah-relief	bas-relief	bannana	banana
baillable	bailable	bannaster	banister

Incorrect	Correct	Incorrect	Correct
banndana	bandanna	bartar	barter
bannish	banish	basett	basset
bannyann	banyan	bashfull	bashful
banquit	banquet	basillisk	basilisk
bantar	banter	basillus	bacillus
bantem	bantam	baskit	basket
banz	banns (wedding)	baskule	bascule
baptizm	baptism	basmotti	basmati
baracks	barracks	baso proffundo	basso profundo
barage	barrage	basoon	bassoon
barbacue	barbecue	bassalt	basalt
barbarrean	barbarian	bassanet	bassinet
barbarrous	barbarous	basse	bass
barbaturrate	barbiturate	bassel	basil (herb)
barck	bark	bassel	basal
barcke	barque (boat)	bassenjy	basenji
barell	barrel	bassic	basic
baren	barren	bassilica	basilica
baricade	barricade	bassin	basin
barister	barrister	Bassque	Basque
barkarole	barcarolle	Basteel	Bastille
barnicle	barnacle	basteon	bastion
barr mittsvah	bar mitzvah	bastird	bastard
barraccuda	barracuda	batche	batch
barrear	barrier	batcheler	bachelor
barrgan	bargain	bateek	batik
barritone	baritone	bathose	bathos
barrkeeper	barkeeper	batt mitsva	bat mitzvah
barrley	barley	Battaan	Bataan
barrometer	barometer	battallion	battalion
barrometric	barometric	battan	batten
barron	baron	battering ram	battering ram
barroque	baroque	batth	bath (noun)

Incorrect	Correct	Incorrect	Correct
battries	batteries	beedle	beadle (order-keeper)
baubble	bauble		
baudy	bawdy	beegle	beagle
Bavarean	Bavarian	beehoove	behoove
Baydekker	Baedeker	beejabbers	bejabbers
Bayjing	Beijing	beelay	belay
baylif	bailiff	Beelzabbub	Beelzebub
bayobabb	baobab	beem	beam
bayonnet	bayonet	beemoan	bemoan
Bayrut	Beirut	beequest	bequest
bayt	bait (lure)	beerate	berate
bayte	bate (hold back)	beeset	beset
bayth	bathe	beesmerch	besmirch
baze	baize	beest	beast
bazzar	bazaar (sale site)	beestow	bestow
beastial	bestial	beetle nut	betel nut
beatel	beetle (bug)	Beetlejuice	Betelgeuse
beatiffic	beatific	beetray	betray
beattitude	beatitude	beever	beaver
beauticean	beautician	befuddel	befuddle
beautyfull	beautiful	begeen	beguine
Beawolf	Beowulf	beger	beggar
becaus	because	beggonia	begonia
beceech	beseech	beginer	beginner
becken	beckon	begining	beginning
becomm	becalm	begruge	begrudge
beday	bidet	beguyle	beguile
bedazzel	bedazzle	behaviour	behavior
bedeked	bedecked	beheemuth	behemoth
bedlem	bedlam	beholdan	beholden
bedraggel	bedraggle	beich	beech (tree)
bedriddan	bedridden	bejou	bijou
beeche	beach	bekeeper	beekeeper

Incorrect	Correct	Incorrect	Correct
beleager	beleaguer	bereeve	bereave
beleave	believe	Berkley, CA	Berkeley, CA
beleef	belief	berme	berm
beleive	believe	bernaze	béarnaise
beligerant	belligerent	Bernooly principle	Bernoulli principle
bell conto	bel canto		
bellacose	bellicose	bernoose	burnoose
bellated	belated	berray	beret
bellch	belch	Berring Sea	Bering Sea
belledonna	belladonna	berryl	beryl
bellfry	belfry	beseige	besiege
belligorancy	belligerency	beserk	berserk
bell-letters	belles-lettres	besteallity	bestiality
bello	bellow	Bethlaham	Bethlehem
bellos	bellows	betrothel	betrothal
belluga	beluga	bett noir	bête noire
bellweather	bellwether	betta	beta
belvadere	belvedere	bettelling	beetling
bemuze	bemuse	bevvel	bevel
benadiction	benediction	bevverage	beverage
beneeth	beneath	bevvy	bevy
benine	benign	bewich	bewitch
benited	benighted	bezzel	bezel
bennafactor	benefactor	bianual	biannual
bennafit	benefit	biarhythm	biorhythm
benneffacent	beneficent	biathalon	biathlon
benneffasence	beneficence	Bib lettuce	Bibb lettuce
benneficial	beneficial	bibbliofile	bibliophile
benneficiary	beneficiary	bibbliography	bibliography
bennevolant	benevolent	bibbulous	bibulous
bennevolence	benevolence	bibliomannia	bibliomania
benzeen	benzene	bicammeral	bicameral
beqweath	bequeath	bicceps	biceps

Incorrect	Correct	Incorrect	Correct
bicentenial	bicentennial	binnaural	binaural
bicussped	bicuspid	binnecle	binnacle
biday	bidet	binoccular	binocular
bienneal	biennial	binommial	binomial
bies	bias	biodegradebel	biodegradable
biet	bight	biohazzard	biohazard
biffurcate	bifurcate	biollogical	biological
bifocle	bifocal	biollogy	biology
biggamous	bigamous	biopsey	biopsy
biggamy	bigamy	biottic	biotic
biggit	bigot	bipartisen	bipartisan
biggitry	bigotry	bipartitte	bipartite
bikker	bicker	bipead	biped
bikkini	bikini	bipoler	bipolar
bilabbial	bilabial	birracial	biracial
bilabong	billabong	bisecter	bisector
bilatteral	bilateral	bisen	bison
bild	build	bisexuel	bisexual
hiliards	billiards	bisicle	bicycle
biline	byline	bisk	bisque
bilinguel	bilingual	biskit	biscuit
bilje	bilge	bissect	bisect
billa-dou	billet-doux	bisstro	bistro
billdungsroman	bildungsroman	bitturn	bittern
billge	bilge	bituminnous	bituminous
billionnaire	billionaire	bivwack	bivouac
billious	bilious	bizantenne	byzantine
billit	billet	bizzare	bizarre (weird)
billo	billow	bladdar	bladder
billyrubin	bilirubin	bladderwirt	bladderwort
bilque	bilk	blahzay	blasé
binarry	binary	blairr	blare
binch	bench	blandishmant	blandishment

Incorrect	Correct	Incorrect	Correct
blanshe	blanch	bluggeon	bludgeon
Blarny Stone	Blarney Stone	blunderbus	blunderbuss
blasphamy	blasphemy	blurte	blurt
blasphemme	blaspheme	boardelo	bordello
blatent	blatant	boaste	boast
blazzen	blazon	boatson	boatswain
blazzer	blazer	bobbalink	bobolink
bleech	bleach	bobbel	bobble
bleek	bleak	boch	botch
bleery	bleary	bochy	bocce
bleet	bleat	bockxite	bauxite
blemmish	blemish	bocoo	beaucoup
blenney	blenny	bodaga	bodega
blesst	blest or blessed	boddis	bodice
		bodken	bodkin
bleugrass	bluegrass	boere	bore (drill, be dull)
blints	blintz		
blite	blight	boerr	boar (male hog)
blitzkreeg	blitzkrieg	boeu	beau
blizzerd	blizzard	Bofort scale	Beaufort scale
bloch	blotch	boggel	boggle
blockaid	blockade	boggey	bogey
blocke	bloc (allied group)	bohemmean	bohemian
		boille	boil
blocke	block square piece)	Boil's law	Boyle's law
		boistarous	boisterous
bloodcurdeling	bloodcurdling	Bojulay	Beaujolais
bloosey	bluesy	bok choey	bok choy
blossum	blossom	boklava	baklava
blote	bloat	boldrope	boltrope
blouzy	blowzy	boline	bowline
blowse	blouse	bolk	balk
bluette	bluet	Bolkans	Balkans

Incorrect	Correct	Incorrect	Correct
bolla	bola	boofont	bouffant
bollder	boulder	boogy	boogie
bolle	boll	bookeeping	bookkeeping
bollero	bolero	Boollean	Boolean
bollicks	bollix	boomarang	boomerang
bollo	bolo	boondocs	boondocks
Bollshoy	Bolshoi	boondoggel	boondoggle
bollster	bolster	Boore War	Boer War
bollurd	bollard	booresh	boorish
bollus	bolus	bootane	butane
Bolshavik	Bolshevik	booy	buoy
Bolshavism	Bolshevism	booyancy	buoyancy
bombadier	bombardier	borbon	bourbon
bomm	balm	boredam	boredom
bon moe	bon mot	borgeoisie	bourgeoisie
bon swar	bonsoir	Borrdoe	Bordeaux
bon vevant	bon vivant	borre	boar (male hog)
bon vowaje	bon voyage	borre	Boer (S. African)
bondible	bondable	borreal	boreal
bonna fida	bona fide	borrough	borough
bonnamie	bonhomie	borrzoy	borzoi
bonndage	bondage	Bosk	Bosc
bonnett	bonnet	bosmotti	basmati
bonnfire	bonfire	botannist	botanist
bonnsigh	bonsai (plant)	botche	bocce
bonnus	bonus	boteak	boutique
bonzai	banzai (Japanese cheer)	botique	boutique
		bott	baht
		bottanical	botanical
boobie	booby	bottulism	botulism
Booda	Buddha	bou	bough
Boodism	Buddhism	bougle	bugle
boodwar	boudoir	boukay	bouquet

Incorrect	Correct	Incorrect	Correct
boul	boll	bravaddo	bravado
boullabase	bouillabaisse	bravary	bravery
boullavard	boulevard	bravvura	bravura
boullion	bouillon (broth)	braye	brae (Scottish hill)
boundry	boundary		
bountious	bounteous	braye	bray (harsh noise)
bourscht	borscht		
bourzhwa	bourgeois	brayle	braille
boutt	bought	braze	braise
bouy	buoy	brazere	brassiere (twin cups)
bouzum	bosom		
bovinne	bovine	brazzen	brazen
bowary	bowery	brazzier	brazier (firepit)
bowdlarize	bowdlerize	brazzile nut	Brazil nut
bowell	bowel	breakedge	breakage
bowey knife	bowie knife	breakible	breakable
bowspritt	bowsprit	breaze	breeze
boycot	boycott	bredth	breadth
boze-arts	beaux-arts	bree	brie
bracelette	bracelet	breeche	breach
brackesh	brackish	breef	brief
brackycephalic	brachycephalic	breethe	breathe (verb)
bradicardea	bradycardia	breeve	breve
bragadoccia	braggadocio	breir	briar (shrub, pipe)
braggert	braggart		
braide	braid	brekfast	breakfast
brambel	bramble	brem	bream (fish)
Brammin	Brahmin	bremm	brim (edge)
brandesh	brandish	breth	breath (noun, air)
brassero	bracero		
braul	brawl	bretheren	brethren
braun recluse	brown recluse	breveary	breviary
braune	brawn	brevvet	brevet

Incorrect	Correct	Incorrect	Correct
brewerey	brewery	brodleaf	broadleaf
bribbery	bribery	broggan	brogan
briches	britches	broggue	brogue
brickabrack	bric-a-brac	broiller	broiler
brickett	briquette	brokerrage	brokerage
bridel	bridal (in regard to a wedding)	bromilliad	bromeliad
		brommide	bromide
bridel	bridle (horse strap)	bronchitus	bronchitis
		Bronks	Bronx
bridgroom	bridegroom	bronschweiger	braunschweiger
brien	brine	brontossaur	brontosaur
briere	brier or briar (prickly plant)	bronz	bronze
		broose	bruise
brige	bridge	broot	bruit
briggade	brigade	broshett	brochette
briggadere	brigadier	broshure	brochure
briggand	brigand	brothal	brothel
brillianse	brilliance	brothe	broth
brindel	brindle	brott	brought
briskit	brisket	brotworst	bratwurst
bristel	bristle	brouny	brownie
Britainnia	Britannia	brouse	browse
brite	bright	broyl	broil
Brittan	Briton (person)	bruche	brooch
brittel	brittle	brucksism	bruxism
Britteny spaniel	Brittany spaniel	bruhaha	brouhaha
Brittian	Britain	brunete	brunette (woman)
Brobdingnaggean	Brobdingnagian		
broch	broach	brunett	brunet (man)
brochet	brochette	Brunzwic stew	Brunswick stew
brockade	brocade	brusk	brusque
brocolli	broccoli	Brussle sprouts	Brussels sprouts
brode	broad	brutallity	brutality

Incorrect	Correct	Incorrect	Correct
brutt	brut	bullge	bulge
bruttle	brutal	bulluck	bullock
bubbaley	bubbly	bullwark	bulwark
bubbel	bubble	bullyen	bullion (gold)
bubonnic	bubonic	bumpken	bumpkin
buccanneer	buccaneer	bundel	bundle
bucher	butcher	bungaloe	bungalow
buckel	buckle	bunnion	bunion
Buckenwalled	Buchenwald	Bunnsen burner	Bunsen burner
buckit	bucket	bunnting	bunting
buckrum	buckram	buoyency	buoyancy
bucksom	buxom	bureaucrassy	bureaucracy
buckwheet	buckwheat	bureaucratteze	bureaucratese
bucollic	bucolic	burgamott	bergamot
Buddah	Buddha	burgandy	burgundy
budgetteer	budgeteer	burgar	burgher (townsperson)
budje	budge		
budjit	budget	burgerr	burger (sandwich)
Budwiser	Budweiser		
buebonnic	bubonic	burgion	burgeon
bufallo	buffalo	burgler	burglar
buffay	buffet (food bar)	buritto	burrito
buffit	buffet (hit)	burjee	burgee
bufoon	buffoon	burlesk	burlesque
buggaboo	bugaboo	burrden	burden
buhwanna	bwana	burrdock	burdock
bulbus	bulbous	burre	burr
bulemmia	bulimia	burrey	bury
bulimmic	bulemic	burrial	burial
bulkee	bulky	burrlap	burlap
bulkhed	bulkhead	burrnish	burnish
bullatin	bulletin	burrnoose	burnoose
bulleon	bullion	burrsitis	bursitis

Incorrect	Correct	Incorrect	Correct
burser	bursar	buyou	bayou
bushle	bushel	buziboddy	busybody
bussken	buskin	buziness	business
bussker	busker	buzouki	bouzouki
bussle	bustle	buzzerd	buzzard
busstier	bustier	buzzward	buzzword
busterd	bustard	bycammerel	bicameral
butonniere	boutonniere	byelawe	bylaw
butterscoch	butterscotch	bylatteral	bilateral
buttler	butler	byoote	butte
buttrass	buttress	bysexuel	bisexual
buttucks	buttocks		

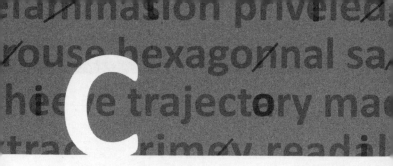

Most Commonly Misspelled Words

- calendar
- careful
- category
- ceiling
- cemetery
- certain
- chief
- citizen
- convenience
- criticize

Incorrect	Correct	Incorrect	Correct
cabaal	cabal	caftann	caftan
cabarray	cabaret	cahutz	cahoots
cabbagge	cabbage	cajolle	cajole
cabballero	caballero	cajollery	cajolery
cabbernay	cabernet	calamory	calamari
cabbinet	cabinet	calcifacation	calcification
cabboodel	caboodle	calcullable	calculable
cabboose	caboose	calcullate	calculate
cabell	cable	calcullator	calculator
cabriolay	cabriolet	calculous	calculus
cabur	caber	calderra	caldera
cacayo	cacao	calender	calendar
cachiatory	cacciatore	caligraffy	calligraphy
cackel	cackle	calimari	calamari
cacktus	cactus	calke	caulk
cacoffany	cacophony	callabash	calabash
cadavver	cadaver	callabrate	calibrate
caddaverus	cadaverous	callabration	calibration
caddenza	cadenza	callah lily	calla lily
caddet	cadet	callamatous	calamitous
caddey	caddie (club carrier)	callamine	calamine
		callamity	calamity
caddey	caddy (tea holder)	callapygean	callipygian
		calldron	cauldron
caddray	cadre	calleef	caliph
caddus	caddis	callefaction	calefaction
cadense	cadence	callends	calends
cadeucious	caduceus	calliber	caliber
cadmeum	cadmium	callico	calico
caern	cairn	calliflower	cauliflower
cafay	café	callipers	calipers
cafay corranery	café coronary	callipso	calypso
caffateria	cafeteria	callisthenics	calisthenics
caffeen	caffeine	callo	callow

Incorrect	Correct	Incorrect	Correct
cassolay	cassoulet	cammise	camise
calloric	caloric	cammpo	campo
callory	calorie	cammshaft	camshaft
callossaty	callosity	Camoo	Camus
callumet	calumet	campane	campaign
calluss	callous (uncaring)	campassino	campesino
		campuss	campus
calluss	callus (thick skin)	cancilation	cancellation
		cancker	canker
Callvery	Calvary	candadate	candidate
calmattive	calmative	canded	candid
caloomneate	calumniate	candel	candle
calsafie	calcify	candellabra	candelabra
calsium	calcium	candleabrum	candelabrum
calumnee	calumny	candore	candor
calv	calve	caniballize	cannibalize
Calvanism	Calvinism	Cann	Cannes
cambar	camber	Cannada	Canada
cambeum	cambium	cannal	canal
camellea	camellia	cannaloni	canneloni
camellion	chameleon	Cannan	Canaan
camera obscurra	camera obscura	cannapay	canapé (snack)
Camerroon	Cameroon	cannapy	canopy (cover)
camm	calm	cannard	canard
camm	cam	cannary	canary
cammaflage	camouflage	cannasta	canasta
Cammalot	Camelot	Cannaveral	Canaveral
cammarodery	camaraderie	cannen	cannon (big gun)
Cammbridge	Cambridge		
cammel	camel	cannen	canon (church rule)
cammera	camera		
cammfer	camphor	cannester	canister
cammicaze	kamikaze	canney	canny
cammio	cameo	cannibel	cannibal

Incorrect	Correct	Incorrect	Correct
cannibiss	cannabis	capitullate	capitulate
cannister	canister	capitullation	capitulation
cannoe	canoe	capoot	kaput
cannonize	canonize	capor	caper
cannto	canto	cappacious	capacious
cannton	canton	cappacity	capacity
canolli	cannoli	cappilary	capillary
canonnic	canonic	cappital	capital
Canoote	Canute	Cappital Hill	Capitol Hill
cansel	cancel	capprice	caprice
canser	cancer	cappricious	capricious
cantalever	cantilever	Cappricorn	Capricorn
cantalope	cantaloupe	cappsize	capsize
Cantaneze	Cantonese	cappstan	capstan
cantankarus	cantankerous	cappture	capture
cantatta	cantata	cappuchin	capuchin
Canterburry	Canterbury	cappybara	capybara
canterr	canter (trot)	capsion	caption
canticul	canticle	capsuel	capsule
cantine	canteen	capsullize	capsulize
cantur	cantor (singer)	captavate	captivate
canulla	cannula	capteous	captious
canvis	canvas (tough cloth)	capter	captor
		captian	captain
canvus	canvass (survey)	captivaty	captivity
		capuccino	cappuccino
canyen	canyon	carabener	carabiner or karabiner (fastener)
capabel	capable		
capabillity	capability		
capan	capon	caraffe	carafe
capilet	caplet	caramelise	caramelize
capitalise	capitalize	carbahydrate	carbohydrate
capitallism	capitalism	carbarrater	carburetor

Incorrect	Correct	Incorrect	Correct
carbarrundem	carborundum	carnidge	carnage
carbean	carbine	carnivvarous	carnivorous
carbon dioxxide	carbon dioxide	carolle	carol (song, sing)
carbon monoxxide	carbon monoxide	Carollinean	Carolinian
carbonifferous	carboniferous	carot	carrot (vegetable)
carbonnara	carbonara	carottid	carotid
carbouy	carboy	caroussle	carousal
carbun	carbon	carpanter	carpenter
carbunkle	carbuncle	carpay diem	carpe diem
carcinnogen	carcinogen	carpcntery	carpentry
carcinnoma	carcinoma	carple	carpal
cardaggan	cardigan	carple tunnell	carpal tunnel
cardemum	cardamom	Carrabean	Caribbean
cardinel	cardinal	Carracas	Caracas
cardiogramm	cardiogram	carrakoo	karakul
cardiollagist	cardiologist	carramba	caramba
cardiollogy	cardiology	carrapace	carapace
cardiovascullar	cardiovascular	carravan	caravan
cardyac	cardiac	carravel	caravel
cardyalgia	cardialgia	carrbide	carbide
carefull	careful	carrear	carrier
carkas	carcass	carreen	careen
carma	karma	carreer	career
carmel	caramel	carress	caress
Carmellite	Carmelite	carret	carat (jewel weight)
carminne	carmine	carret	caret (insert mark)
Carnagie	Carnegie	carret	carrot (vegetable)
carnasion	carnation	carret	karat (gold measure)
carnel	carnal		
carnellean	carnelian		
carneval	carnival		
carnevore	carnivore		

Incorrect	Correct	Incorrect	Correct
carrian	carrion	cassarole	casserole
carribeaner	carabiner	cassavva	cassava
carricature	caricature	casscade	cascade
carrige	carriage	cassein	casein
carrilon	carillon	cassino	casino
carrob	carob	cassoc	cassock
carroll	carrel (library nook)	cassowarry	cassowary
		casst	cast
carrom	carom	casstaway	castaway
carrosel	carousel (carnival ride)	casstrate	castrate
		cassual	casual
carrouse	carouse (go carousing)	cassualty	casualty
		cassuistry	casuistry
carrousel	carousal (wild outing)	cassus belli	casus belli
		castagate	castigate
carrton	carton	castannets	castanets
cart blansh	carte blanche	castar bean	castor bean
cartalaginous	cartilaginous	castel	castle
cartell	cartel	Castillean	Castilian
Cartezzean	Cartesian	castratto	castrato (singular)
cartilege	cartilage		
cartredge	cartridge	castratty	castrati (plural)
cartune	cartoon	catail	cattail
casehardin	caseharden	catallepsy	catalepsy
casett	cassette	catatonnic	catatonic
cashay	cachet	cataulba	catalpa
cashe	cache	catharsus	catharsis
casheer	cashier	cathartick	cathartic
cashue	cashew	cathater	catheter
caskit	casket	cathedrel	cathedral
cass system	caste system	cathoad	cathode
cassaba	casaba	Catholicizm	Catholicism
Cassanndra	Cassandra	Cathollic	Catholic
Cassanova	Casanova	cator	cater

Incorrect	Correct	Incorrect	Correct
catspaw	cat's-paw	cavvalcade	cavalcade
cattabolism	catabolism	cavvallier	cavalier
cattachresis	catachresis	cavvalry	cavalry (horses)
cattaclysm	cataclysm	cavvaty	cavity
cattacomb	catacomb	cavvendish	cavendish
cattagorical	categorical	cavviar	caviar
cattagory	category	cavvil	cavil
cattakism	catechism	cavvitation	cavitation
cattalist	catalyst	cawcus	caucus
cattalize	catalyze	cayanne	cayenne
cattalog	catalog	caymann	caiman
cattalytick	catalytic	Caymann Islands	Cayman Islands
cattameran	catamaran	Cayne	Cain
cattamount	catamount	caynine	canine
cattanery	catenary	cayolin	kaolin
cattapault	catapult	cayoose	cayuse
cattar	catarrh	cayotte	coyote
cattarack	cataract	caypo	capo
cattastrophe	catastrophe	Cayro	Cairo
catterpiller	caterpillar	cayson	caisson
catterwall	caterwaul	cazbar	casbah
cattrafoil	quatrefoil	cazzmere	cashmere
Caucassian	Caucasian	Ceaser	Caesar
caudel	caudal	Ceaserian	Caesarean
caudeyo	caudillo	ceasurra	caesura
cause cellebra	cause célèbre	cecuum	cecum
caushious	cautious	ceddar	cedar
causion	caution	ceddila	cedilla
caussal	causal	ceelia	cilia
caustick	caustic	ceelocanth	coelacanth
cauterrize	cauterize	ceese	cease
cautionnary	cautionary	ceffalopod	cephalopod
cauzeway	causeway	ceilling	ceiling
cavernus	cavernous	celabration	celebration

Incorrect	Correct	Incorrect	Correct
cellabacy	celibacy	ceptic	septic
cellebrate	celebrate	cerabellum	cerebellum
cellebraties	celebrities	Cerberrus	Cerberus
cellebrent	celebrant	ceremonnial	ceremonial
cellebrity	celebrity	cerial	serial (series)
celler	cellar	Cerino de Berzerak	Cyrano de Bergerac
cellerity	celerity		
cellesteal	celestial	cerramic	ceramic
cellibate	celibate	cerrebrel	cerebral
Cellseus	Celsius	cerrebrum	cerebrum
celluller	cellular	cerremony	ceremony
cellullite	cellulite	cerriel	cereal (food)
cellullose	cellulose	certafiable	certifiable
celophane	cellophane	certatude	certitude
cematary	cemetery	certefy	certify
Cennozoic	Cenozoic	certificatte	certificate
cennser	censor	certin	certain
cenotaff	cenotaph	cerviccal	cervical
censership	censorship	cervics	cervix
censhur	censure	ceseum	cesium
censoreus	censorious	cessasion	cessation
centagrade	centigrade	cessta	cesta
centameter	centimeter	cetasean	cetacean
centapede	centipede	cetollogy	cetology
centenial	centennial	Cezzane	Cezanne
centennarean	centenarian	chabley	chablis
centerbord	centerboard	chaf	chaff
centerrary	centenary	chalcadony	chalcedony
centore	centaur	challace	chalice
centrafuge	centrifuge	challange	challenge
centrallize	centralize	chamberlin	chamberlain
centrepittal	centripetal	chamfur	chamfer
centriffugal	centrifugal	chammomeal	chamomile
cephallick	cephalic	chammy	chamois

Incorrect	Correct	Incorrect	Correct
champaine	champagne	charrisma	charisma
champian	champion	charritable	charitable
chanell	channel	charrwoman	charwoman
changable	changeable	charry	chary
changelling	changeling	chartroos	chartreuse
chansan	chanson	charzhe d'affaires	charge d'affaires
chansary	chancery	chased	chaste
chansellor	chancellor	chasse lounge	chaise longue
chanticlear	chanticleer	chassten	chasten
chantuse	chanteuse	chassy	chassis
chao	ciao	chastety	chastity
chaoss	chaos	chaslize	chastise
chaottic	chaotic	Chatenooga	Chattanooga
chaperron	chaperone	chatteau	chateau
chaplin	chaplain	chattle	chattel
chapparel	chaparral	chattobriand	chateaubriand
chappel	chapel	chauvanism	chauvinism
chappou	chapeau	chayf	chafe
charaty	charity	chazable	chasuble
charcole	charcoal	chazm	chasm
chardonay	chardonnay	cheaf	chief
chardosh	czardas	Checkoslovakia	Czechoslovakia
chargable	chargeable	checkrain	checkrein
charjay d'affairs	charge d'affaires	chedder	cheddar
Charlamain	Charlemagne	cheechy	chichi
charleton	charlatan	cheenos	chinos
charnal	charnel	cheepe	cheap (low-cost, stingy)
Charolay	Charolais		
charoscurro	chiaroscuro	cheepskate	cheapskate
charracter	character	cheerfull	cheerful
charracteristic	characteristic	cheet	cheat
charracterize	characterize	cheeta	cheetah
charrade	charade	chef-d'ouver	chef-d'oeuvre
charriot	chariot	cheffon	chiffon

Incorrect	Correct	Incorrect	Correct
chein	chine	chiffarobe	chifforobe
chello	cello	chiggar	chigger
chemastry	chemistry	chil facter	chill factor
chembly	chimney	chili rallano	chile relleno
chemmical	chemical	chillblanes	chilblains
chemmin de fir	chemin de fer	Chille	Chile
chemmise	chemise	chilli con carney	chili con carne
chemmist	chemist	chimmera	chimera
chemmotherrapy	chemotherapy	chimpansy	chimpanzee
chenchilla	chinchilla	chinkapin	chinquapin
chennin blank	chenin blanc	chints	chintz
chenook	chinook	chintzey	chintzy
cherchay la fomme	cherchez la femme	Chipandale	Chippendale
		chipmonk	chipmunk
chern	churn	Chippawah	Chippewa
cherrish	cherish	chirromansee	chiromancy
Cherrokee	Cherokee	chirropracter	chiropractor
cherroot	cheroot	chirropractick	chiropractic
cherrub	cherub	Chissom	Chisholm
cherrup	chirrup	chitllngs	chitterlings
Chesire	Cheshire	chitten	chitin
chesse pie	chess pie	chizle	chisel
chessnut	chestnut	chloraphil	chlorophyll
Chesspeak	Chesapeake	choccablok	chockablock
chevran	chevron	chockful	chockfull
chevvalier	chevalier	chocolit	chocolate
Cheyanne	Cheyenne	choer	chore
chez longue	chaise longue	choffeur	chauffeur
chicannary	chicanery	choire	choir
chickel	chicle	chok	chock
chickenpocks	chickenpox	chokra	chakra
chickery	chicory	Choktaw	Choctaw
chickpee	chickpea	cholesterrol	cholesterol
chieftane	chieftain	chollera	cholera

Incorrect	Correct	Incorrect	Correct
cholleric	choleric	churchey	churchy
Chommski	Chomsky	Churchhill	Churchill
chooreezo	chorizo	churllish	churlish
choot	chute	chuttnee	chutney
chop sooey	chop suey	chutzzpa	chutzpah
chorragraph	choreograph	cicadda	cicada
chorrister	chorister	ciccatrix	cicatrix
chorrus	chorus	Cicerro	Cicero
chortel	chortle	ciggar	cigar
chou-chou	chowchow	ciggerette	cigarette
chouder	chowder	cignett	cygnet
chow main	chow mein	cillantro	cilantro
chozen	chosen	cimball	cymbal
chrisanthamum	chrysanthemum	Cimmaron	Cimarron
Chrismass	Christmas	cinammon	cinnamon
chrisote	creosote	Cincinatti	Cincinnati
chrissalis	chrysalis	Cinderrela	Cinderella
chrissen	christen	cinemmatograffy	cinematography
Christean	Christian	cinnema	cinema
Christianaty	Christianity	cinnema veritay	cinema verite
chrom	chrome	cintch	cinch
chromasome	chromosome	circadean	circadian
chromattic	chromatic	circcatry	circuitry
chromiam	chromium	circkits	circuits
chrommatography	chromatography	circomscribed	circumscribed
chronalogical	chronological	circuitus	circuitous
chronical	chronicle	circuler	circular
chronnic	chronic	circullation	circulation
chronograf	chronograph	circumcission	circumcision
chronollogy	chronology	circumferense	circumference
chuckel	chuckle	circumlocusion	circumlocution
chucker	chukker (polo)	circumnavvigate	circumnavigate
chuggalugg	chug-a-lug	circumsize	circumcise
chukkar	chukar (bird)	circumspec	circumspect

Incorrect	Correct	Incorrect	Correct
circumstanses	circumstances	clarevoyence	clairvoyance
circumstatiel	circumstantial	clarrinet	clarinet
circumvint	circumvent	clarrit	claret
circuss	circus	classafy	classify
cirhossis	cirrhosis	classasist	classicist
cirkit	circuit	classick	classic
cirrcumflecks	circumflex	classisism	classicism
cirrcumscribe	circumscribe	clau hammar	claw hammer
cirrocumulous	cirrocumulus	claustraphobia	claustrophobia
cirrostrattus	cirrostratus	claut	clout
cirrous	cirrus	clauze	clause
cisturn	cistern	clavez	claves
citrick	citric	clavicord	clavichord
citronnela	citronella	clavvicle	clavicle
citrous	citrus	clayle	clayey
cittadell	citadel	claymor	claymore
cittation	citation	clearity	clarity
cittazen	citizen	clearrence	clearance
civillian	civilian	cleavver	cleaver
civillity	civility	cleek	clique
civily	civilly	cleenze	cleanse
civvet	civet	cleeshay	cliché
civvic	civic	cleet	cleat
civvilization	civilization	cleevage	cleavage
civvilize	civilize	cleeve	cleave
clabboard	clapboard	cleff	clef
clairvoyent	clairvoyant	cleff	cleft
clak	claque	cleff pallate	cleft palate
clame	claim	clemattis	clematis
clammarous	clamorous	clemmancy	clemency
clammor	clamor	clemmant	clement
clams cassino	clams casino	clennse	cleanse
clandestin	clandestine	clergie	clergy
clareon	clarion	clerrastory	clerestory

Incorrect	Correct	Incorrect	Correct
clerrasy	clerisy	clouthe	clothe
clerrical	clerical	clumsey	clumsy
clevver	clever	clusster	cluster
clevvis	clevis	coadajutent	coadjutant
cliant	client	coagguelate	coagulate
clientell	clientele	coaggulant	coagulant
cliffhangar	cliffhanger	coalle	coal
climacterric	climacteric	coallition	coalition
climactick	climactic	Coalmann stove	Coleman stove
climatollogy	climatology	coamming	coaming
climete	climate	coan	koan
climmax	climax	coapse	copse
climmed	climbed	coastel	coastal
clinche	clinch (fasten, hug)	coate	cote (shed)
		coatty	coati
clinicle	clinical	coaxeal	coaxial
clinisian	clinician	cobbalt	cobalt
clinnic	clinic	cobbel	cobble
clintch	clench (close tightly)	cobblar	cobbler
		cobura	cobra
clitorus	clitoris	cocanut	coconut
clochur	cloture	coccoon	cocoon
cloey	cloy	cockamamey	cockamamie
cloistir	cloister	cockatryce	cockatrice
cloke	cloak	cockelburr	cocklebur
cloo	clew	cocketeal	cockatiel
cloo	clue	cocknee	cockney
closehawled	close-hauled	cockroche	cockroach
closh	cloche	cockscomb	coxcomb
closset	closet	cocksix	coccyx
clossure	closure	cocksun	coxswain
clothear	clothier	cockus	coccus
clotheng	clothing	codda	coda
cloun	clown	coddacil	codicil

Incorrect	Correct	Incorrect	Correct
coddafy	codify	cojensy	cogency
coddger	codger	cojito urgo sum	cogito ergo sum
codecks	codex		
codene	codeine	cojjatate	cogitate
COE-BOLL	COBOL	cokain	cocaine
coefficiant	coefficient	cokeel	coquille
coelesce	coalesce	cokette	coquette
coerse	coerce	colaborrate	collaborate
coersion	coercion	colate	collate
coetus	coitus	colatteral	collateral
coetus interruptas	coitus interruptus	coldslaw	coleslaw
		cole chisel	cold chisel
coff	cough	coleague	colleague
coffen	coffin	colegean	collegian
coffeure	coiffeur (hairdresser)	collde	collide
		colission	collision
coffey	coffee	collacate	collocate
cognazance	cognizance	collafon	colophon
cognision	cognition	collagin	collagen
cognizent	cognizant	collanade	colonnade
cognoman	cognomen	collandar	colander
cohabbit	cohabit	Collarado	Colorado
coheer	cohere	collaratura	coloratura
coherance	coherence	collazhe	collage
cohezion	cohesion	collectabals	collectibles
cohoe	coho	collectavism	collectivism
cohones	cojones	coller	collar
cohourt	cohort	collerd	collard
coi	coy (shy)	collery	colliery
coi	koi (fish)	colley	collie
coiffere	coiffure	collic	colic
coinscedance	coincidence	collige	college
coinside	coincide	colliseum	coliseum
Cointro	Cointreau	collon	colon

Incorrect	Correct	Incorrect	Correct
collone	cologne	commazar	commissar
collonise	colonize	commedia d'el arte	commedia dell'arte
collonnel	colonel		
collony	colony	commedian	comedian
colloquee	colloquy	commediene	comedienne (female)
colloquiel	colloquial		
colloquilizm	colloquialism	commedy	comedy
collor	choler	commendasion	commendation
colloring	coloring	commense	commence
collosal	colossal	commensel	commensal
collossus	colossus	commensement	commencement
collostomy	colostomy	commensurit	commensurate
colloyd	colloid	commentery	commentary
collum	column	commerse	commerce
Collumbia	Columbia	commersial	commercial
Collumbus	Columbus	commersialize	commercialize
collushion	collusion	commestible	comestible
collyer	collier	commical	comical
collyform	coliform	commiscion	commission
Comanchee	Comanche	commisery	commissary
combanation	combination	committ	commit
combattent	combatant	commity	comity
combustable	combustible	commodaty	commodity
combusteon	combustion	commonallity	commonality
comemmorate	commemorate	commondant	commandant
comensurrable	commensurable	commondeer	commandeer
comfortible	comfortable	commontater	commentator
comingle	commingle	commosion	commotion
comiserate	commiserate	commrade	comrade
comissioner	commissioner	communacable	communicable
comittee	committee	communer	commoner
comittment	commitment	communicay	communiqué
commador	commodore	communiterian	communitarian
commandmant	commandment	communizm	communism

Incorrect	Correct	Incorrect	Correct
communnal	communal	complane	complain
communwealth	commonwealth	complant	complaint
commuppense	comeuppance	complasence	complaisance
commutater	commutator	complecks	complex
comode	commode	complection	complexion
comodeous	commodious	complexaty	complexity
compack	compact	complicasion	complication
compackter	compactor	complience	compliance
compadray	compadre	complient	compliant
compannion	companion	complimentery	complimentary
compansate	compensate	complissity	complicity
comparrable	comparable	componant	component
comparrative	comparative	compossite	composite
comparrison	comparison	compoze	compose
compartmint	compartment	compozure	composure
compasino	campesino	comprahend	comprehend
compasion	compassion	comprahensible	comprehensible
compasition	composition	comprahension	comprehension
compatable	compatible	compresion	compression
compeling	compelling	comprize	comprise
compell	compel	comptroler	comptroller
compendeum	compendium	compullsive	compulsive
compensible	compensable	compulsary	compulsory
competance	competence	compuncion	compunction
competative	competitive	compus	compass
compillation	compilation	computarize	computerize
complacate	complicate	computasion	computation
complacensy	complacency	comquat	kumquat
complainent	complainant	comu	coma
complament	complement (part of a whole)	comunication	communication
		comutose	comatose
complament	compliment (praise)	concabine	concubine
		concatennation	concatenation
complamentary	complementary	concavvity	concavity

Incorrect	Correct	Incorrect	Correct
conceed	concede	confecsionery	confectionery
conceptualise	conceptualize	confeddaracy	confederacy
concertena	concertina	confederrit	confederate
concessionair	concessionaire	confesser	confessor
concherto	concerto	confessionel	confessional
concievable	conceivable	confetty	confetti
concloosion	conclusion	confidense	confidence
concocksion	concoction	confidintially	confidentially
concommitant	concomitant	configurration	configuration
concordence	concordance	confir	confer
concordent	concordant	confirmasion	confirmation
concreet	concrete	confiskatory	confiscatory
concupascent	concupiscent	conflasion	conflation
concupisance	concupiscence	conflic	conflict
concurr	concur	confligration	conflagration
concurranse	concurrence	confluance	confluence
concusion	concussion	conformasion	conformation
condament	condiment	conformaty	conformity
condasend	condescend	confrantation	confrontation
condasension	condescension	confrer	confrere
condem	condemn	confuscate	confiscate
condemnasion	condemnation	Confuscius	Confucius
conder	condor	Confusianism	Confucianism
condiscion	condition	confuzion	confusion
condoit	conduit	congennial	congenial
condolense	condolence	congennital	congenital
condominnium	condominium	congerries	congeries
conduccion	conduction	conglommerate	conglomerate
conducter	conductor	Congoe	Congo
condusive	conducive	congosenty	cognoscenti
confabbulate	confabulate	congradulate	congratulate
confadant	confidant	congragant	congregant
conarance	conference	congragasion	congregation
confeccion	confection	congragate	congregate

Incorrect	Correct	Incorrect	Correct
congretationallism	congregationalism	consanant	consonant
congruance	congruence	consangwin	consanguine
congruety	congruity	consangwinity	consanguinity
conie	coney	consaquense	consequence
conipsion	conniption	consciencious	conscientious
conjeal	congeal	conscrip	conscript
conjeccure	conjecture	conseal	conceal
conjegate	conjugate	conseat	conceit
conjer	conjure	conseccutive	consecutive
conjoine	conjoin	conseed	concede
conjuggel	conjugal	conselut	consulate
conjuncion	conjunction	consentrasion	concentration
conjunctivitus	conjunctivitis	consentrate	concentrate
Connastoga	Conestoga	consentric	concentric
connasur	connoisseur	consentual	consensual
connatation	connotation	conseption	conception
connclave	conclave	conseptual	conceptual
conncourse	concourse	consequensial	consequential
Conneticut	Connecticut	conserge	concierge
connexion	connection	consern	concern
connfidential	confidential	conservatore	conservator
connflate	conflate	conservatorry	conservatory
connga	conga (dance)	conservency	conservancy
connifer	conifer	conservitizm	conservatism
connifferus	coniferous	consession	concession
connivence	connivance	conshous	conscious
connsort	consort	consice	concise
connubiel	connubial	considerasion	consideration
conote	connote	consience	conscience
conquistidore	conquistador	consient	consent
conqure	conquer	consieve	conceive
conqwest	conquest	consillatory	conciliatory
consacrate	consecrate	consinement	consignment
consalation	consolation	consistancy	consistency

Incorrect	Correct	Incorrect	Correct
consistantly	consistently	contatta	cantata
consollidate	consolidate	contects	context
consolling	consoling	contempararry	contemporary
consommay	consommé	contemporanious	contemporaneous
consortiom	consortium	contemptous	contemptuous
consoul	console	contentuous	contentious
conspectis	conspectus	contenuo	continuo
conspiccuous	conspicuous	contestent	contestant
conspirasy	conspiracy	contextuel	contextual
conspirrator	conspirator	contigguous	contiguous
constabel	constable	contimpt	contempt
constabullery	constabulary	contimptible	contemptible
constallation	constellation	continance	continence
constapate	constipate	continentel	continental
constatution	constitution	contingancy	contingency
constency	constancy	contingeant	contingent
constittuant	constituent	contingince	contingence
constituancy	constituency	continnual	continual
constrane	constrain	continnum	continuum
constrant	constraint	continnuous	continuous
constricsion	constriction	continuaty	continuity
constricter	constrictor	contoor	contour
constru	construe	contorsionist	contortionist
construcsion	construction	contrabasoon	contrabassoon
consturnation	consternation	contracsion	contraction
consubstancial	consubstantial	contracter	contractor
consull	consul	contractuel	contractual
consummer	consumer	contradic	contradict
consummit	consummate	contradistincsion	contradistinction
contageon	contagion	contraltoe	contralto
contageous	contagious	contrapsion	contraption
contamanent	contaminant	contrapuntel	contrapuntal
contamminate	contaminate	contrarean	contrarian
contane	contain	contrarywise	contrariwise

Incorrect	Correct	Incorrect	Correct
contraseptive	contraceptive	convoi	convoy
contratemps	contretemps	convolluted	convoluted
contraveen	contravene	convultion	convulsion
contraversial	controversial	cookaracha	cucaracha
contraversy	controversy	coolent	coolant
contravert	controvert	cooly	coolly
contreban	contraband	coom granno salis	cum grano salis
contribusion	contribution	coomin	cumin
contributorry	contributory	coomulative	cumulative
contrivence	contrivance	coomulus	cumulus
contumaly	contumely	cooparate	cooperate
contumescious	contumacious	coopela	cupola
contumplate	contemplate	coopon	coupon
contussion	contusion	coorary	curare
conundram	conundrum	coordanate	coordinate
convalessence	convalescence	cooscoos	couscous
convalution	convolution	cooticle	cuticle
convay	convey	copeing saw	coping saw
convayence	conveyance	Copenhaggen	Copenhagen
conveccion	convection	copeous	copious
convecks	convex	Copernacus	Copernicus
conveen	convene	coppasetic	copacetic
convence	convince	copp-out	cop-out
conveniance	convenience	coppra	copra
convennient	convenient	coppula	copula
convensional	conventional	coppulate	copulate
convergance	convergence	coppywriter	copywriter
conversent	conversant	copullative	copulative
convertable	convertible	copywright	copyright
converzion	conversion	corbell	corbel
convicsion	conviction	cordadge	cordage
convint	convent	cordan	cordon
convirge	converge	cordan blue	cordon bleu
convivvial	convivial	cordaroy	corduroy

Incorrect	Correct	Incorrect	Correct
cordavan	cordovan	correl	coral
cordeal	cordial	correspondant	correspondent
corect	correct	corrgy	corgi
corellation	correlation	corriculum vitay	curriculum vitae
corellative	correlative	corrigendam	corrigendum
corespondense	correspondence	Corrintheans	Corinthians
coretex	cortex	Cornish	Cornish
coriddor	corridor	corrobarate	corroborate
cormarant	cormorant	corrola	corolla
corneesh	corniche	corrona	corona
corness	cornice	corronation	coronation
cornett	cornet (horn)	corroner	coroner
cornia	cornea	corronet	coronet (crown)
cornucoppea	cornucopia	corrps	corpse
corodde	corrode	corrsage	corsage
corpass dilecti	corpus delicti	corrset	corset
corporial	corporeal	corruptibel	corruptible
corporrate	corporate	corruscate	coruscate
corprell	corporal	corsare	corsair
corpulant	corpulent	corse	coarse
corpullence	corpulence	cortasone	cortisone
corpus collosum	corpus callosum	cortazhe	cortege
corpussle	corpuscle	cort-marshall	court-martial
corr	corps	corupt	corrupt
corragated	corrugated	coruption	corruption
corrageous	courageous	corvet	corvette
corralate	correlate	cosher	kosher
corrale	chorale	cosmanaut	cosmonaut
corrall	corral (horse pen)	cosmapolitan	cosmopolitan
		cosmatology	cosmetology
corrall	coral (as in reef)	cosmettic	cosmetic
corranery	coronary	cossecant	cosecant
corraspond	correspond	cossign	cosign (sign together)
correda	corrida		

Incorrect	Correct	Incorrect	Correct
cossine	cosine (math term)	coutch	couch
		coverege	coverage
cossite	cosset	covnent	covenant
cotage	cottage	covurt	covert
cotanjent	cotangent	covveat	caveat
cotary	coterie	covverlet	coverlet
cotchaneal	cochineal	cowardiss	cowardice
cottaleydon	cotyledon	cowery	cowrie
cottan	cotton	cowtow	kowtow
cottanmouth	cottonmouth	cowwer	cower
cottar pin	cotter pin	crackel	crackle
cottileon	cotillion	cradell	cradle
cou day graaz	coup de grace	cradensials	credentials
cou daytah	coup d'état	craneal	cranial
cougger	cougar	craneum	cranium
cought	caught	crapullence	crapulence
coul	cowl	crapullent	crapulent
counsell	counsel (advise, lawyer)	crashindo	crescendo
		crauw	craw
counsil	council (group)	cravan	craven
countarpoise	counterpoise	cravass	crevasse
counterculcher	counterculture	cravatte	cravat
counterfit	counterfeit	crayun	crayon
counterpropossal	counterproposal	cread	creed
countersine	countersign	creal	creel
countertennor	countertenor	creap	creep
countervale	countervail	creap paper	crepe paper
countnence	countenance	creascion	creation
countryfied	countrified	creast	crest
couplett	couplet	createen	creatine
courrage	courage	creater	creator
courrier	courier	creationnism	creationism
courtiere	courtier	creativvity	creativity
courtizan	courtesan	creayfish	crayfish

Incorrect	Correct	Incorrect	Correct
creddulus	credulous	criminnal	criminal
crediter	creditor	criminollogy	criminology
creditible	creditable	crimpson	crimson
creece	crease	crinnalin	crinoline
creedence	credence	criogenics	cryogenics
creedo	credo	crippel	cripple
creeky	creaky	criptick	cryptic
creemate	cremate	criptography	cryptography
creeole	creole	crispley	crisply
Creesus	Croesus	Crissendom	Christendom
cremanes	cremains	crissis	crisis
cremaslon	cremation	cristaline	crystalline
cremetorium	crematorium	cristall	crystal
cremp	crimp	criteeque	critique
cremson	crimson	criterea	criteria (plural)
crenge	cringe	criterian	criterion (singular)
crengle	cringle		
crennalated	crenelated	critisizm	criticism
crepe mertle	crape myrtle	crittasize	criticize
creppuscular	crepuscular	crittic	critic
crepz	crepes	critticle	critical
creshe	crèche	croan	crone
cressent	crescent	crobarr	crowbar
cressfallen	crestfallen	croccadile	crocodile
cretacious	cretaceous	croch	crotch
crettanism	cretinism	crocke	crock
creviss	crevice	crockerry	crockery
crewal	crewel	crocuss	crocus
crewit	cruet	crokay	croquet
cribbige	cribbage	croke	croak
crickit	cricket	crokett	croquette
crim de la crim	crème de la crème	Crones disease	Crohn's disease
		croney	crony
criminallity	criminality	croneyism	cronyism

Incorrect	Correct	Incorrect	Correct
croodity	crudity	cuddel	cuddle
croodutay	crudités	cudgil	cudgel
crool	cruel	cueue	queue
croopeay	croupier	culchure	culture
crootan	crouton	cull de sack	cul de sac
croshay	crochet	cullinery	culinary
crossant	croissant	cullpret	culprit
croud	crowd	culltavator	cultivator
croud	crude	cullturel	cultural
croun	crown	cullvert	culvert
croutch	crouch	culmenate	culminate
Crow-magnin	Cro-Magnon	culpabel	culpable
cruch	crutch	culturelly	culturally
crucibel	crucible	cumbarsome	cumbersome
crucificcion	crucifixion	cumbshaw	cumshaw
crucks	crux	cummerbunn	cummerbund
cruddenza	credenza	cumpass	compass
crudulaty	credulity	cuncoct	concoct
cruize	cruise	cuneyform	cuneiform
crummie	crummy	Cupey	Kewpie (doll)
crushall	crucial	cupfull	cupful
crusifix	crucifix	cuppidity	cupidity
crussade	crusade	curdel	curdle
crussafy	crucify	cureater	curator
crustascion	crustacean	cureossity	curiosity
cruth	crwth	cureous	curious
cryp	crypt	curfue	curfew
crystalize	crystallize	curicullum	curriculum
cuaff	coif	curit	curate
cubbacle	cubicle	curlycue	curlicue
cubbic	cubic	curmuggion	curmudgeon
cubeism	cubism	currable	curable
cubeit	cubit	currunt	current (flow, or up to date)
cuckled	cuckold		

Incorrect	Correct	Incorrect	Correct
currunt	currant (shrub or its berry)	cuttlery	cutlery
		cuvven	coven
currantly	currently	cuvvet	covet
currensy	currency	cuvvy	covey
currey	curry	cuzzen	cozen
currint	currant (dried berry)	cybernettics	cybernetics
		cycal	cycle
currser	cursor	cyclick	cyclic
currsive	cursive	cycloan	cyclone
currtail	curtail	cyclopps	cyclops
cursary	cursory	cyder	cider
curteous	courteous	cyenide	cyanide
curtesy	courtesy	cylender	cylinder
curtian	curtain	cylindracle	cylindrical
curtsey	curtsy (bow)	cynansure	cynosure
curvasious	curvaceous	cynasizm	cynicism
curviture	curvature	cynick	cynic
cushen	cushion	cypruss	cypress (tree)
cusstady	custody	cypruss	Cyprus (city, island)
cussterd	custard		
custamary	customary	cystascope	cystoscope
custoddean	custodian	cystick fibbrosus	cystic fibrosis
custommise	customize	cytollagy	cytology
cutanious	cutaneous	czair	czar
cutless	cutlass	Czechaslovokia	Czechoslovakia
cuttelbone	cuttlebone		

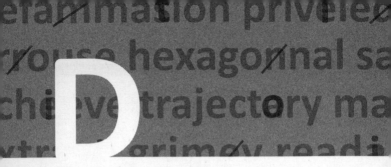

Most Commonly Misspelled Words

- daffodil
- dandelion
- definitely
- desperate
- develop
- difference
- dilemma
- disappoint
- discipline
- during

Incorrect	Correct	Incorrect	Correct
da facto	de facto	daredevvil	daredevil
da Vinchi	da Vinci	Darjeeling	Darjeeling
dabbel	dabble	darrear	derriere
dabue	debut	darring	daring
Dacarte	Descartes	Darwanism	Darwinism
dacktolollagy	dactylology	Darwinnean	Darwinian
dacore	decor	dashbord	dashboard
daffadil	daffodil	dasheeky	dashiki
dafft	daft	dashhound	dachshund
dagerrotype	daguerreotype	dasterd	dastard
daggar	dagger	dattive	dative
dailly	daily	daun	dawn
dain	deign	daus	dais
dairey	dairy	davvenport	davenport
dallea	dahlia	davvit	davit
Dallmation	Dalmatian	dawdel	dawdle
dallyanse	dalliance	Daycron	Dacron
damisk	damask	daydo	dado
dammage	damage	dayta	data
Dammascus	Damascus	daytont	detente
dammnation	damnation	dayze	daisy
damsal	damsel	de fackto	de facto
danamond	denouement	de rigguer	de rigueur
dandel	dandle	deacide	deicide
dandriff	dandruff	deactavate	deactivate
dandylion	dandelion	Deadalus	Daedalus
dangerus	dangerous	deafication	deification
dannish	danish (pastry)	deaft	deft
dansure	danseur	debait	debate
danty	dainty	debarck	debark
dappar	dapper	debatible	debatable
dappel	dapple	debbit	debit
daquiri	daiquiri	debbonair	debonair
Dardanneles	Dardanelles	debboshee	debauchee

Incorrect	Correct	Incorrect	Correct
debbutant	debutante	decimmel	decimal
debillitate	debilitate	decinneal	decennial
debillity	debility	decission	decision
deboch	debauch	deckstrose	dextrose
debochery	debauchery	declair	declare
debockle	debacle	declame	declaim
debree	debris	declammation	declamation
debunck	debunk	declammatory	declamatory
decadant	decadent	declanation	declination
decadense	decadence	declassafy	declassify
decaffanated	decaffeinated	declassay	déclassé
decaid	decade	declenchion	declension
decapatate	decapitate	decleration	declaration
decathalete	decathlete	decliene	decline
decathalon	decathlon	declivaty	declivity
Deccalogue	Decalogue	decoad	decode
deccanter	decanter	decollatzhe	decolletage
deccapod	decapod	decommision	decommission
deccarous	decorous	decompresion	decompression
deccorate	decorate	decontammanate	decontaminate
deccoy	decoy	decorrum	decorum
deccree	decree	decouppage	decoupage
deceazed	deceased	decrashindo	decrescendo
decedant	decedent	decreese	decrease
deceitfull	deceitful	decreppit	decrepit
decellarate	decelerate	decrie	decry
decend	descend	deddacate	dedicate
decensy	decency	dedeuce	deduce
decentrallize	decentralize	dedline	deadline
decepsion	deception	dedlock	deadlock
deciet	deceit	deductabel	deductible
decieve	deceive	deeafy	deify
decifer	decipher	deeaty	deity
decilitter	deciliter	deecon	deacon

Incorrect	Correct	Incorrect	Correct
deefenbackia	dieffenbachia	defient	defiant
deefer	defer	defillade	defilade
deeism	deism	definately	definitely
deele	dele (delete)	definnative	definitive
de-emphacize	de-emphasize	defishency	deficiency
deemure	demure	deflassion	deflation
deen	dean	defleccion	deflection
de-escallate	de-escalate	deflour	deflower
deevious	devious	defolleate	defoliate
defalt	default	defollient	defoliant
defammasion	defamation	defraude	defraud
defammatory	defamatory	defunkt	defunct
defe	deaf	defusse	defuse
defecktive	defective	Degah	Degas
defeet	defeat	deggredation	degradation
defendent	defendant	deggustation	degustation
defennestration	defenestration	deginnerit	degenerate
defensabble	defensible	degousse	degauss
deffacate	defecate	dehidrate	dehydrate
deffacation	defecation	dehiss	dehisce
deffacit	deficit	dehummitify	dehumidify
deffalcation	defalcation	deisel	diesel
deffanission	definition	deja vue	déjà vu
deffening	deafening	dejeccion	dejection
defferanse	deference	dekahedron	decahedron
defferential	deferential	dekal	decal
defferment	deferment	dekay	decay
deffile	defile	delamminate	delaminate
defformation	deformation	delectible	delectable
defformaty	deformity	deleerious	delirious
deffray	defray	delibberate	deliberate
defibralation	defibrillation	delicattesen	delicatessen
defibrallate	defibrillate	delinnyate	delineate
defience	defiance	delinquant	delinquent

Incorrect	Correct	Incorrect	Correct
delinquinsy	delinquency	demmagogy	demagogy
delireum tremmens	delirium tremens	demmagraphics	demographics
delishous	delicious	demmalicion	demolition
dellagate	delegate	demmented	demented
dellaquesce	deliquesce	demmimond	demimonde
dellaterious	deleterious	demmonstrate	demonstrate
Dellaware	Delaware	demmonstration	demonstration
delletion	deletion	demmotick	demotic
Dellfick	Delphic	demmurije	demurrage
dellicacy	delicacy	demoballize	demobilize
delliver	deliver	demollish	demolish
delliverance	deliverance	demonick	demonic
dellphineum	delphinium	demurr	demur
dellta	delta	demurre	demure
delltoid	deltoid	dendriet	dendrite
dellusion	delusion	dengo	dingo
delluxe	deluxe	deniabillity	deniability
delooshe	deluge	dennagrate	denigrate
dem summ	dim sum	dennazen	denizen
demagnettize	demagnetize	denniable	deniable
demanize	demonize	denniele	denial
demarcasion	demarcation	dennotation	denotation
demarkate	demarcate	denominasion	denomination
demateriallize	dematerialize	denomminator	denominator
demeaner	demeanor	denoomond	denouement
demensia	dementia	denounse	denounce
demerrit	demerit	denounsing	denouncing
demijon	demijohn	densetty	density
demillaterise	demilitarize	dentafrise	dentifrice
demin	demon	dentasion	dentation
demisstafy	demystify	denunciasion	denunciation
demize	demise	deoderent	deodorant
demmacrat	democrat	departmentel	departmental
demmagog	demagogue	dependanse	dependence

Incorrect	Correct	Incorrect	Correct
dependansy	dependency	derrogatory	derogatory
dependant	dependent	dervesh	dervish
depersonnalise	depersonalize	desallanation	desalination
depillatory	depilatory	descripsion	description
depleet	deplete	desegreggate	desegregate
deplorrible	deplorable	desendent	descendant (from specific lineage) descendent (moving downward)
depoppulate	depopulate		
deportasion	deportation		
deportmant	deportment		
depossatory	depository	desensatise	desensitize
depposition	deposition	desent	descent (going down)
deppracate	deprecate		
deppravation	deprivation	desent	decent (suitable)
deppth	depth	desiduous	deciduous
depravvity	depravity	desirabel	desirable
depreciasion	depreciation	desparate	desperate
depressent	depressant	desparation	desperation
depresser	depressor	despare	despair
depressian	depression	despatism	despotism
deputee	deputy	desperrado	desperado
deracinnation	deracination	despiccable	despicable
derailler	derailleur	despize	despise
deregullation	deregulation	despoile	despoil
derk	dirk	despondansy	despondency
dermabrassion	dermabrasion	despondant	despondent
dermatitas	dermatitis	despottic	despotic
dermatollogy	dermatology	desput	despot
dernea cri	dernier cri	dessacant	desiccant
derrack	derrick	dessacate	desiccate
derralict	derelict	dessacrate	desecrate
derrisive	derisive	dessart	dessert (sweet)
derrivation	derivation	dessibel	decibel
derrivative	derivative	dessimate	decimate
derrizion	derision		

Incorrect	Correct	Incorrect	Correct
dessurt	desert (sandy)	devoyd	devoid
destabellize	destabilize	devvastate	devastate
destanation	destination	devvastating	devastating
destatute	destitute	devvotee	devotee
destatution	destitution	dewey	dewy
destiney	destiny	dextarous	dexterous
destroier	destroyer	dexterraty	dexterity
deswatude	desuetude	dextrus	dexterous
detanee	detainee	dezidderatum	desideratum
deteccion	detection	deziner	designer
detension	detention	dezist	desist
detereorate	deteriorate	dezzalate	desolate
determinnant	determinant	dezzignate	designate
determinnation	determination	dezzultory	desultory
deterrance	deterrence	diabollic	diabolic
deterrgent	detergent	diacrittical	diacritical
detoxafy	detoxify	diadd	dyad
detraccion	detraction	diadim	diadem
detrament	detriment	diaffanus	diaphanous
detrytus	detritus	diaframm	diaphragm
dettanate	detonate	diaggonal	diagonal
dettanation	detonation	diagnoce	diagnose
dettanator	detonator	diagnosstic	diagnostic
detter	deter	diagnosus	diagnosis
dettor	debtor	dialate	dilate
deus ex maccana	deus ex machina	diallasis	dialysis
deva	diva	diallectic	dialectic
devalluation	devaluation	diallogue	dialogue
devallue	devalue	diamater	diameter
devane	devein	diametricly	diametrically
devellop	develop	diannthos	dianthus
devient	deviant	diaphannus	diaphanous
devinity	divinity	diarrea	diarrhea
devitallize	devitalize	diarry	diary

Incorrect	Correct	Incorrect	Correct
diaspara	diaspora	digerrydoo	didgeridoo
diatonnic	diatonic	digestable	digestible
diattribe	diatribe	diggress	digress
dibbel	dibble	digitallas	digitalis
dibeteze	diabetes	digittal	digital
dibettic	diabetic	dignafied	dignified
diccion	diction	dignafy	dignify
dich	ditch	digniterry	dignitary
dichottamy	dichotomy	dignitty	dignity
dicktum	dictum	digressian	digression
dicotyleedan	dicotyledon	dijestion	digestion
dictatorreal	dictatorial	dilappidated	dilapidated
dictionerry	dictionary	dillagence	diligence
diddapper	didapper	dillatonte	dilettante
diddy	ditty	dillatory	dilatory
didjit	digit	dillema	dilemma
diedactic	didactic	dillusion	delusion
diellect	dialect	dillute	dilute
diepole	dipole	diluveal	diluvial
dier straights	dire straits	dimmanusion	diminution
dierrasis	dieresis	dimmenish	diminish
dieterry	dietary	dimminishing	diminishing
diey	dye	dimminsion	dimension
diffacult	difficult	dimminutive	diminutive
diffadence	diffidence	dimond	diamond
diffadent	diffident	dimpel	dimple
differance	difference	dinasty	dynasty
differant	different	dinggy	dinghy
differencial	differential	dinjy	dingy
differenciate	differentiate	dinnasour	dinosaur
difftheria	diphtheria	dinnete	dinette
diffthong	diphthong	diociss	diocese
diffuce	diffuse	Dioneesean	Dionysian
diffuseon	diffusion	dioramma	diorama

Incorrect	Correct	Incorrect	Correct
dioxxin	dioxin	disconsert	disconcert
diper	diaper	discontinnuence	discontinuance
diphthirea	diphtheria	discouragment	discouragement
diplamat	diplomat	discource	discourse
diplamatic	diplomatic	discreat	discreet (circumspect)
diplomma	diploma		
diplommacy	diplomacy	discrepensy	discrepancy
diploppia	diplopia	discression	discretion
dipploy	deploy	discriet	discrete (of separate parts
dippthong	diphthong		
dipsomannia	dipsomania	discrimmanation	discrimination
diptick	diptych	discrimminate	discriminate
directary	directory	discurrage	discourage
directer	director	discurrsive	discursive
dirj	dirge	discurteous	discourteous
dirndel	dirndl	disdane	disdain
dirragible	dirigible	disect	dissect
disabillaty	disability	disembowwel	disembowel
disadvantageos	disadvantageous	disent	dissent (disagree)
disapate	dissipate		
disapline	discipline	disent	descent (going down)
disastarous	disastrous		
disatisfaction	dissatisfaction	disertation	dissertation
disatisfied	dissatisfied	disfuncsion	dysfunction
disberse	disburse	disgorje	disgorge
discipal	disciple	disgruntel	disgruntle
disciplinery	disciplinary	disguize	disguise
disclame	disclaim	disharmany	disharmony
disclossure	disclosure	dishevval	dishevel
discoggraphy	discography	dishonnorable	dishonorable
discoller	discolor	disinfectent	disinfectant
discommfit	discomfit	disintagrate	disintegrate
discomode	discommode	diske	disk, disc
disconsallit	disconsolate	dislexxia	dyslexia

Incorrect	Correct	Incorrect	Correct
dislexxic	dyslexic	dissabille	dishabille
dislocate	dislocate	dissable	disable
disloyaltey	disloyalty	dissabuze	disabuse
dismantel	dismantle	dissadent	dissident
dismel	dismal	dissadvantige	disadvantage
dismissel	dismissal	dissagree	disagree
disociation	dissociation	dissagreeable	disagreeable
disorgannized	disorganized	dissalusion	disillusion
dispair	despair	dissalute	dissolute
disparrige	disparage	dissanance	dissonance
disparrity	disparity	dissanent	dissonant
disparrut	disparate	dissaplinarian	disciplinarian
dispassionit	dispassionate	dissapline	discipline
dispence	dispense	dissapoint	disappoint
dispensasion	dispensation	dissaray	disarray
dispensible	dispensable	dissassemble	disassemble
dispeptic	dyspeptic	dissaster	disaster
dispise	despise	disscord	discord
dispite	despite	disscordent	discordant
displazia	dysplasia	disscredit	discredit
displeazure	displeasure	disscus	discus
disposess	dispossess	dissease	disease
disposible	disposable	dissembark	disembark
dispossition	disposition	dissembody	disembody
dispozel	disposal	dissenchant	disenchant
disprapportionate	disproportionate	dissencion	dissension
disproporsion	disproportion	dissengenuous	disingenuous
dispurse	disperse	dissentary	dysentery
dispurzion	dispersion	dissequalibrium	disequilibrium
disputent	disputant	dissern	discern
disquallify	disqualify	dissestablish	disestablish
disreggard	disregard	dissfigure	disfigure
disrepputable	disreputable	dissgorge	disgorge
dissabedience	disobedience	dissharten	dishearten

Incorrect	Correct	Incorrect	Correct
dissimble	dissemble	distressfull	distressful
dissiminate	disseminate	distribbute	distribute
dissimmilar	dissimilar	distributer	distributor
dissinclination	disinclination	districk	district
dissinsentive	disincentive	distructive	destructive
dissinter	disinter	disturbence	disturbance
dissjunct	disjunct	disunnity	disunity
dissmay	dismay	dithyram	dithyramb
dissorderly	disorderly	dittoe	ditto
dissorient	disorient	diuressis	diuresis
disspell	dispel	diuretick	diuretic
dissplease	displease	diurnel	diurnal
dissputible	disputable	divann	divan
dissrespectful	disrespectful	diversafy	diversify
disstaff	distaff	diversatty	diversity
disstinctive	distinctive	divertamento	divertimento
dissuede	dissuade	diverticullitus	diverticulitis
distell	distal	diverzionery	diversionary
distenguish	distinguish	divestature	divestiture
disterb	disturb	divirge	diverge
distick	distich	divissable	divisible
distilation	distillation	divission	division
distillary	distillery	divorse	divorce
distimper	distemper	divorsee	divorcée (woman), or divorcé (man)
distincsion	distinction		
distind	distend	divour	devour
distingay	distingue	divout	devout
distink	distinct	divurse	diverse
distoppia	dystopia	divurt	divert
distrabution	distribution	divvadend	dividend
distrac	distract	divvergent	divergent
distraccion	distraction	divversion	diversion
distrafee	dystrophy	divvide	divide
distraut	distraught	divvination	divination

Incorrect	Correct	Incorrect	Correct
divvine	divine	dommano	domino
divvisor	divisor	dommesticate	domesticate
divvulge	divulge	dommestick	domestic
dizzie	dizzy	domminatricks	dominatrix
doat	dote	dommineering	domineering
dobarmen	doberman	domminence	dominance
dobb	daub	dommineon	dominion
dobbson fly	dobsonfly	Don Keyhotey	Don Quixote
dobrow	Dobro	donacion	donation
doccument	document	donky	donkey
dockit	docket	donnate	donate
docksun	dachshund	donnebrook	donnybrook
doctorette	doctorate	donseuss	danseuse
doctranair	doctrinaire	doobeous	dubious
doctrin	doctrine	dooce	deuce
documentery	documentary	doodel	doodle
docummentation	documentation	doolap	dewlap
dodeccahedron	dodecahedron	doop	dupe
dodje	dodge	dooplex	duplex
dogerrel	doggerel	doorjam	doorjamb
dogmattick	dogmatic	doovay	duvet
doilly	doily	doppamine	dopamine
doldrems	doldrums	Dopplar affect	Doppler effect
dolful	doleful	doppleganger	doppelganger
dollfin	dolphin	dorke	dork
Dolli Lomma	Dalai Lama	Dorkus	Dorcas
dollicocephalic	dolichocephalic	dormar	dormer
dollorous	dolorous	dormatory	dormitory
dolmin	dolmen	dorment	dormant
dolop	dollop	dorry	dory
domestissity	domesticity	dorsel	dorsal
dominnasion	domination	dossage	dosage
dommacile	domicile	dossea	dossier
dommain	domain	dossent	docent

Incorrect	Correct	Incorrect	Correct
dossil	docile	drawwar	drawer
dosydo	dos-a-dos	dreadlox	dreadlocks
dot-mattrix	dot-matrix	dredd	dread
dottage	dotage	dredje	dredge
dotter	daughter	drednaut	dreadnaught
doublitt	doublet	dreem	dream
doue	dough (pastry)	dreery	dreary
doue	doe (deer)	dreggs	dregs
doughnutt	doughnut	dreidle	dreidel
dountless	dauntless	driad	dryad
doure	dour	dribbel	dribble
dout	doubt	driffwood	driftwood
doutfull	doubtful	drinch	drench
douze	douse	drivvel	drivel
dovecoat	dovecote	drivven	driven
dovetale	dovetail	drizzel	drizzle
downrite	downright	droa de sinyer	droit du seigneur
dowwager	dowager	droag	drogue
dowwal	dowel	droan	drone
dowwery	dowry	drockma	drachma
doxollagy	doxology	drole	droll
draconean	draconian	drollary	drollery
draggonfly	dragonfly	dromma	drama
dramattic	dramatic	drommadery	dromedary
drammaticly	dramatically	drooid	druid
drammatis personey	dramatis personae	droppsy	dropsy
		drossofila	drosophila
drammatize	dramatize	drothers	druthers
drammaturgy	dramaturgy	droun	drown
drane	drain	droup	droop
dranije	drainage	drouse	drowse
draparry	drapery	drout	drought
drasstick	drastic	drugerry	drudgery
drauss	dross	drunkeness	drunkenness

Incorrect	Correct	Incorrect	Correct
drunkerd	drunkard	dungion	dungeon
drussazh	dressage	dunn	dun
Duay Bible	Douay Bible	dunse	dunce
dubble	double	duoddanem	duodenum
Dubbye	Dubai	duodecimmal	duodecimal
duble-entonde	double-entendre	duplacate	duplicate
dubloon	doubloon	duplissaty	duplicity
Duch treet	Dutch treat	durasion	duration
duckt	duct	durible	durable
ducktile	ductile	durramater	dura mater
dudgeun	dudgeon	durress	duress
dueçe	dcuce	durring	during
duell	dual (twin)	durth	dearth
duell	duel (fight)	dutchess	duchess
duena	duenna	dutchy	duchy
dueo	duo	dutifull	dutiful
Dueteranomy	Deuteronomy	duzzen	dozen
duett	duet	Dvorshock	Dvorák
duffal	duffel	dwel	dwell
duggong	dugong	dwendel	dwindle
duh zhour	du jour	dworff	dwarf
dukkat	ducat	dyeng	dyeing
dulcit	dulcet	dynamizm	dynamism
dullerd	dullard	dynammick	dynamic
dulsammer	dulcimer	dynne	dyne
dulsit	dulcet	dyode	diode
dumbdumb	dumdum	Dyonesius	Dionysus
dumbell	dumbbell	dyool	duel (contest)
dungerees	dungarees		

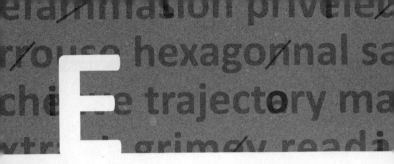

Most Commonly Misspelled Words

- easily
- either
- embarrass
- environment
- exaggerate
- exercise
- existence
- expect
- experience
- explanation

Incorrect	Correct	Incorrect	Correct
E Cheng	I Ching	ecctoplasm	ectoplasm
e plurribus unam	e pluribus unum	eccumenical	ecumenical
E. colli	E coli	eche	etch
eaclare	eclair	eckdizziast	ecdysiast
eaggel	eagle	ecko	echo
eagger	eager	eckolallia	echolalia
eaite	eight	ecksimma	eczema
eal	eel	eclampsea	eclampsia
ean	eon	eclay	éclat
eardrumm	eardrum	eclectick	eclectic
earee	eerie	Ecleeseastes	Ecclesiastes
earing	earring	eclippse	eclipse
earley	early	ecollogy	ecology
earnast	earnest	econnomy	economy
earne	earn	econommical	economical
earthe	earth	ecse homo	ecce homo
earthernwear	earthenware	ecsintricity	eccentricity
earthqwake	earthquake	ecstattic	ecstatic
earwigg	earwig	ecstissy	ecstasy
easally	easily	ectomorff	ectomorph
easle	easel	eday feecks	idée fixe
easment	easement	eddema	edema
Eastar	Easter	eddentate	edentate
eatible	eatable	eddict	edict
eaze	ease	eddiface	edifice
eb	ebb	eddification	edification
Ebbonics	Ebonics	eddify	edify
ebbony	ebony	eddition	edition (publication)
ebulliant	ebullient		
eccinaccia	echinacea	eddition	addition (math)
eccocide	ecocide	edditor	editor
eccosystem	ecosystem	editorial	editorial
eccru	ecru	edducable	educable
eccsintric	eccentric	edducate	educate

Incorrect	Correct	Incorrect	Correct
edducater	educator	efuljent	effulgent
edeuce	educe	egadd	egad
editorrialize	editorialize	egalitarrian	egalitarian
eech	each	egg fu yung	egg foo yong
eegis	aegis	eggnogg	eggnog
eeke out	eke out	eggo	ego
eemcee	emcee	eggotist	egotist
eepay	epee	eggress	egress
eequine	equine	eggret	egret
Eerie Canal	Erie Canal	eggs Bennadict	eggs Benedict
eermark	earmark	egomannia	egomania
eeves	eaves	egosentric	egocentric
efase	efface	egotisticcal	egotistical
efeet	effete	egotizm	egotism
efemminate	effeminate	egreegious	egregious
effacasious	efficacious	Egypsion	Egyptian
effacassy	efficacy	Eiffle Tower	Eiffel Tower
effagy	effigy	eightteen	eighteen
effarvese	effervesce	eigth	eight
effarvesent	effervescent	eigth	eighth
effeck	effect	einsconse	ensconce
effectsual	effectual	Einstine	Einstein
effemerra	ephemera	Eissenhowar	Eisenhower
effemerral	ephemeral	eithere	either
efficiant	efficient	ejecshun	ejection
efficiensy	efficiency	ejeculate	ejaculate
effimanacy	effeminacy	ejject	eject
effluant	effluent	ekidna	echidna
effluince	effluence	El Neenio	El Niño
effluvea	effluvia	elaborrate	elaborate
effluveum	effluvium	elamentery	elementary
effrontry	effrontery	elastick	elastic
effucive	effusive	elastissity	elasticity
effulginse	effulgence	eldar	elder

Incorrect	Correct	Incorrect	Correct
eldarly	elderly	ellavator	elevator
elecsion	election	ellbow	elbow
electorrate	electorate	ellect	elect
electorrel	electoral	ellectorel	electoral
electrafy	electrify	ellectracute	electrocute
electralite	electrolyte	ellectrocardiagram	
electrallasis	electrolysis		electrocardiogram
electramagnet	electromagnet	ellectromagnatism	
electrissaty	electricity		electromagnetism
electroenseffalogram		ellectron	electron
	electroencephalogram	ellegy	elegy
electronnic	electronic	ellevate	elevate
eleet	elite	elleven	eleven
eleetizm	elitism	ellide	elide
elfe	elf	ellisit	elicit
elfes	elves	ellission	elision
elimmanate	eliminate	ellixer	elixir
elipse	ellipse	ellocusion	elocution
elipsis	ellipsis	ellon	elan
elipticle	elliptical	ellongate	elongate
Elizzabethen	Elizabethan	ellope	elope
ellafantiasis	elephantiasis	elloquent	eloquent
ellagance	elegance	ellusive	elusive
ellagant	elegant	eluciddate	elucidate
ellagible	eligible	emansipate	emancipate
ellajiac	elegiac	emansipation	emancipation
ellament	element	emascalate	emasculate
ellamossanery	eleemosynary	embalism	embolism
elland	eland	embarass	embarrass
ellaphent	elephant	embarck	embark
ellapse	elapse	embassey	embassy
ellaquense	eloquence	embelish	embellish
ellate	elate	embezzel	embezzle
ellavation	elevation	embibe	imbibe

Incorrect	Correct	Incorrect	Correct
emblamatic	emblematic	emmploy	employ
emblazzen	emblazon	emmu	emu
emblim	emblem	emmunity	immunity
emboddiment	embodiment	emollumint	emolument
embolm	embalm	emp	imp
embrase	embrace	empass	impasse
embrio	embryo	emperical	empirical
embroader	embroider	emperror	emperor
embryonick	embryonic	empethy	empathy
embur	ember	emphacise	emphasize
emergint	emergent	emphatick	emphatic
emfacema	emphysema	emplanted	implanted
emfassis	emphasis	emporeum	emporium
emfattic	emphatic	emullate	emulate
emmaciate	emaciate	emullsify	emulsify
emmanance	eminence	emullsion	emulsion
emmanate	emanate	en rout	en route
emmanent	eminent	enammel	enamel
emmarold	emerald	enammored	enamored
emmasary	emissary	encapsullate	encapsulate
emmbargo	embargo	enceffalitis	encephalitis
emmend	emend	enchallada	enchilada
emmendasion	emendation	enchantement	enchantment
emmeratus	emeritus	enclossure	enclosure
emmergancy	emergency	encommeum	encomium
emmerge	emerge	encompess	encompass
emmergence	emergence	encourrage	encourage
emmery	emery	encript	encrypt
emmetick	emetic	encroche	encroach
emmigrate	emigrate	encumbar	encumber
emmision	emission	encumberence	encumbrance
emmit	emit	encyclopeddic	encyclopedic
emmoliant	emollient	encyclopedea	encyclopedia
emmotion	emotion	endemmick	endemic

Incorrect	Correct	Incorrect	Correct
endevvor	endeavor	ennough	enough
endivve	endive	ennrich	enrich
endokrin	endocrine	ennsue	ensue
endomorf	endomorph	ennsure	ensure
endorce	endorse	ennunciate	enunciate
endorphan	endorphin	ennuresis	enuresis
endou	endow	enorrmus	enormous
endowmint	endowment	enovation	innovation
endurense	endurance	enquest	inquest
enfallade	enfilade	enrapsher	enrapture
enfeebelled	enfeebled	enrole	enroll
enfranchize	enfranchise	enschrine	enshrine
engauge	engage	ensconse	ensconce
engaugement	engagement	ensiddious	insidious
engendar	engender	ensillage	ensilage
engourge	engorge	ensinn	ensign
engroce	engross	ensinnuate	insinuate
enhanse	enhance	ensomble	ensemble
enigmattic	enigmatic	enstagate	instigate
enjaneer	engineer	ensullar	insular
enject	inject	ensurgence	insurgence
enlightenmant	enlightenment	ensurgints	insurgents
enliten	enlighten	entager	integer
enmitty	enmity	entale	entail
enn masse	en mass	entamollogy	entomology
ennama	enema	entatty	entity
ennate	innate	enterprize	enterprise
ennergetic	energetic	entertane	entertain
ennergized	energized	enthoosiast	enthusiast
ennervate	enervate	enthroll	enthrall
ennervated	enervated	enthuziasm	enthusiasm
enngrave	engrave	entigrate	integrate
ennigma	enigma	entise	entice
ennormatey	enormity	entittle	entitle

Incorrect	Correct	Incorrect	Correct
entra acte	entr'acte	epittamy	epitome
entranse	entrance	eponnamous	eponymous
entrappment	entrapment	epoxxie	epoxy
entrappy	entropy	eppacure	epicure
entraprenure	entrepreneur	eppademic	epidemic
entreet	entreat	eppagram	epigram
entregue	intrigue	eppalepptic	epileptic
entrensic	intrinsic	eppalepsy	epilepsy
entreppid	intrepid	eppallet	epaulet
entrills	entrails	eppasene	epicene
entrinch	entrench	eppic	epic
entrude	intrude	eppicanthus	epicanthus
entruder	intruder	eppicenter	epicenter
enuff	enough	eppicurian	epicurean
enummerate	enumerate	eppidermis	epidermis
enureses	enuresis	eppifany	epiphany
envalope	envelope	eppiglotas	epiglottis
envestigator	investigator	eppigramatic	epigrammatic
envie	envy	eppigraph	epigraph
envirans	environs	eppilog	epilogue
environement	environment	Eppiscopal	Episcopal
envirenmental	environmental	eppisoddic	episodic
envissage	envisage	eppisode	episode
envizion	envision	eppistemollogy	epistemology
envyous	envious	eppitaph	epitaph
enwee	ennui	eppitheleum	epithelium
enzime	enzyme	eppizootic	epizootic
eonn	eon	eppoch	epoch
epadural	epidural	eqquate	equate
ephemmera	ephemera	equallize	equalize
ephemmeral	ephemeral	equanimmity	equanimity
epipheny	epiphany	equassion	equation
Episcopallean	Episcopalian	equatter	equator
episle	epistle	equel	equal

Incorrect	Correct	Incorrect	Correct
equestrean	equestrian	erronius	erroneous
equilatteral	equilateral	errosion	erosion
equillibrium	equilibrium	errotic	erotic
equinimmaty	equanimity	errudite	erudite
equinnox	equinox	errudition	erudition
equinoctil	equinoctial	erruption	eruption
equipmant	equipment	ersotz	ersatz
equipoze	equipoise	erstwile	erstwhile
equitasion	equitation	escalater	escalator
equitorreal	equatorial	escallate	escalate
equittable	equitable	escapegoat	scapegoat
equitty	equity	escargo	escargot
equivelance	equivalence	eschatollogy	eschatology
equivelant	equivalent	escheet	escheat
equivvocate	equivocate	eschoo	eschew
erace	erase	escritorre	escritoire
eraddacate	eradicate	escro	escrow
erand	errand	escutchon	escutcheon
erectille	erectile	eshallon	echelon
erganommics	ergonomics	Eskamo	Eskimo
ergg	erg	espeanaje	espionage
ergott	ergot	especialy	especially
ermin	ermine	espedrill	espadrille
erra	era	Esperranto	Esperanto
erratta	errata	esplannade	esplanade
errattic	erratic	espoussel	espousal
errect	erect	esquirre	esquire
errection	erection	essateric	esoteric
erremite	eremite	esscapaid	escapade
errent	errant	esscort	escort
errganomic	ergonomic	essencial	essential
errly	early	essense	essence
errode	erode	essentielly	essentially
errogenous	erogenous	essophagus	esophagus

Incorrect	Correct	Incorrect	Correct
esspalia	espalier	euivoccal	equivocal
essthetics	aesthetics	euker	euchre
esstranged	estranged	eullagize	eulogize
estabblish	establish	eullogy	eulogy
establishmantarianism		eunuck	eunuch
	establishmentarianism	euphamism	euphemism
establishmentarean		euphoneum	euphonium
	establishmentarian	euphonius	euphonious
establishmint	establishment	euphonnic	euphonic
estamate	estimate	euphorria	euphoria
esteam	esteem	euphorric	euphoric
estheete	aesthete	euphuizm	euphuism
esthettic	esthetic	Eurapean	European
estragen	estrogen	Eurasean	Eurasian
estras	estrus	eurika	eureka
estuerry	estuary	Europpe	Europe
et cettera	et cetera	eustashean	eustachian
etable	edible	evaccuate	evacuate
eternel	eternal	evaid	evade
eternitty	eternity	evalluate	evaluate
ethere	ether	evanesince	evanescence
etherial	ethereal	evangellical	evangelical
ethick	ethic	evangellism	evangelism
ethnacentrism	ethnocentrism	evangellist	evangelist
ethneck	ethnic	evangellize	evangelize
etiollogy	etiology	evappurate	evaporate
etoufay	etouffee	evassion	evasion
ettamology	etymology	evenning	evening
ettaquette	etiquette	eventfull	eventful
ettude	etude	eventfuly	eventfully
etymollogy	etymology	eventuallity	eventuality
eucaliptus	eucalyptus	eventualy	eventually
Eucherist	Eucharist	eventuel	eventual
eugennics	eugenics	evisserate	eviscerate

Incorrect	Correct	Incorrect	Correct
evoccative	evocative	excrament	excrement
evvalution	evolution	excrusiate	excruciate
Evverglades	Everglades	excurseon	excursion
evvergreen	evergreen	excusible	excusable
evvidence	evidence	excusitory	excusatory
evvident	evident	exellance	excellence
evvidential	evidential	exemplery	exemplary
evvince	evince	exercize	exercise
evvinescent	evanescent	exersism	exorcism
ex catheedra	ex cathedra	exfoleate	exfoliate
ex officeo	ex officio	exhallation	exhalation
ex poste facto	ex post facto	exhaltation	exaltation
exactatude	exactitude	exhibbit	exhibit
exactoe	X-acto	exhibbition	exhibition
exagirate	exaggerate	exhillarate	exhilarate
exalation	exhalation	exhoust	exhaust
examinnation	examination	exibit	exhibit
exasperrate	exasperate	exibition	exhibition
exasserbait	exacerbate	exigesis	exegesis
Excallaber	Excalibur	exilarate	exhilarate
excalpate	exculpate	eximplar	exemplar
excavasion	excavation	existance	existence
excell	excel	existentualism	existentialism
excellense	excellence	exogammy	exogamy
excellsior	excelsior	exoskelton	exoskeleton
exchecker	exchequer	expadition	expedition
excitible	excitable	expaditious	expeditious
exclame	exclaim	expance	expanse
exclammation	exclamation	expantion	expansion
exclammatory	exclamatory	expatriot	expatriate
excloosive	exclusive	expeate	expiate
excluseon	exclusion	expeck	expect
excommunnicate	excommunicate	expectasion	expectation
excorriate	excoriate	expectency	expectancy

Incorrect	Correct	Incorrect	Correct
expectent	expectant	exseed	exceed
expecterate	expectorate	exsept	excerpt
expediancy	expediency	exsess	excess
expediant	expedient	exsize	excise
expell	expel	extemporraneous	extemporaneous
expence	expense	extemporrize	extemporize
expendature	expenditure	extenct	extinct
expendible	expendable	extenguish	extinguish
experament	experiment	extennsive	extensive
experamental	experimental	extennuate	extenuate
experamentation	experimentation	exterminnate	exterminate
expergate	expurgate	exterminnator	exterminator
experiense	experience	externallize	externalize
experteece	expertise	externel	external
expidite	expedite	exterrior	exterior
explacate	explicate	extincion	extension
explaination	explanation	extole	extol
explane	explain	extorsion	extortion
explannatory	explanatory	extrac	extract
explative	expletive	extracate	extricate
explissit	explicit	extraccion	extraction
exploratorry	exploratory	extracurriculer	extracurricular
explossion	explosion	extramarrital	extramarital
exponensial	exponential	extranious	extraneous
exponnent	exponent	extraordanary	extraordinary
exportasion	exportation	extrapollate	extrapolate
expositorry	expository	extrasensary	extrasensory
expozition	exposition	extraterrestreal	extraterrestrial
expozure	exposure	extravagganza	extravaganza
expresion	expression	extravegance	extravagance
expressionizm	expressionism	extravegant	extravagant
expropreate	expropriate	extraversion	extroversion
expullsion	expulsion	extravurt	extrovert
exquizit	exquisite	extredite	extradite

Incorrect	Correct	Incorrect	Correct
extredition	extradition	exxile	exile
extreem	extreme	exxonerate	exonerate
extremizm	extremism	exxorbitent	exorbitant
extremmity	extremity	exxorcise	exorcise
extrensic	extrinsic	exxorsist	exorcist
exuberrance	exuberance	exxort	exhort
exurben	exurban	exxortation	exhortation
exxact	exact	exxotic	exotic
exxacute	execute	exxpansive	expansive
exxacution	execution	exxploit	exploit
exxadus	exodus	exxploitation	exploitation
exxalt	exalt	exxpress	express
exxecrable	execrable	exxpunge	expunge
exxecutive	executive	exxtant	extant
exxemplify	exemplify	exxtend	extend
exxempt	exempt	exxude	exude
exxemption	exemption	exxult	exult
exxert	exert	exxurbia	exurbia
exxigency	exigency	eyefull	eyeful

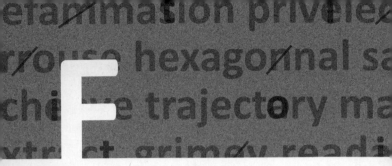

Most Commonly Misspelled Words

- fallible
- familiar
- festival
- fictitious
- finally
- foreign
- forty
- fundamentalist
- furniture
- futility

Incorrect	Correct	Incorrect	Correct
fabalist	fabulist	fallter	falter
fabbul	fable	fallus	phallus
fabracation	fabrication	falselly	falsely
fabrick	fabric	falsety	falsity
fabulus	fabulous	familliar	familiar
faccalty	faculty	familliarity	familiarity
facillation	facilitation	familliarize	familiarize
facillities	facilities	fammen	famine
facsimmaly	facsimile	fammish	famish
facsion	faction	fammus	famous
facsual	factual	fane	feign
factoous	factious	fanfair	fanfare
facter	factor	fannatic	fanatic
factorreal	factorial	fannaticism	fanaticism
factotem	factotum	fanntail	fantail
fadd	fad	fanntan	fantan
fadied	faded	fansifull	fanciful
fadish	faddish	fansy	fancy
fai	fey	fant	faint
faillure	failure	fantacy	fantasy
fairry	fairy	fantastick	fantastic
faise	faze	fantazia	fantasia
faithfull	faithful	fantisize	fantasize
fakeer	fakir	faraggo	farrago
fallable	fallible	farkelberry	farkleberry
fallaceous	fallacious	farmasootical	pharmaceutical
fallafel	falafel	farmasy	pharmacy
fallasy	fallacy	farrad	farad
fallcon	falcon	Farrenhite	Fahrenheit
fallick	phallic	farrina	farina
falloe	fallow	farro	faro
fallopean tube	fallopian tube	farrthingale	farthingale
fallsetto	falsetto	farse	farce
fallsify	falsify	farsiccal	farcical

Incorrect	Correct	Incorrect	Correct
Farsie	Farsi	featt	fiat
fasceal	facial	feazable	feasible
fasciest	fascist	feazzanse	feasance
fascinnate	fascinate	februle	febrile
fasecious	facetious	Febuary	February
fashea	fascia	fech	fetch
fashionible	fashionable	feddayean	fedayeen
fasillity	facility	fedderal	federal
fasset	facet	fedderation	federation
fassil	facile	fedorra	fedora
fassination	fascination	feebil	feeble
fassizm	fascism	feecal	fecal
fassod	façade	feecees	feces
fasstidius	fastidious	feecund	fecund
fatallity	fatality	feecundaty	fecundity
fate accomplee	fait accompli	feeline	feline
fatefull	fateful	feelty	fealty
fatel	fatal	feenominal	phenomenal
fathum	fathom	feetal	fetal
fatid	fated	feeture	feature
fatteague	fatigue	feetuss	fetus
fattuity	fatuity	feifdom	fiefdom
fattuous	fatuous	feind	fiend
fau pah	faux pas	feindish	fiendish
faunn	fawn	feirce	fierce
faunna	fauna	fekless	feckless
fauset	faucet	fellany	felony
Faustean	Faustian	fellasheo	fellatio
faver	favor	fellicitation	felicitation
favorible	favorable	fellicitious	felicitous
feansay	fiancé or fiancée	fellicity	felicity
fearfulley	fearfully	fellon	felon
feasco	fiasco	fellonious	felonious

Incorrect	Correct	Incorrect	Correct
fellspar	feldspar	fetherwaite	featherweight
fem fatalle	femme fatale	fett	fete
femminine	feminine	fetta cheese	feta cheese
femurre	femur	fettaccine	fettuccine
fenn	fen (swamp)	fettar	fetter
fenn	fin (on a fish)	fettid	fetid
fennder	fender	fettish	fetish
fennell	fennel	feudel	feudal
fennestration	fenestration	feuze	fuse
fennugreak	fenugreek	feverrish	feverish
fenommanon	phenomenon	fewse	fuse
fent	feint	feyted	feted
feord	fjord	fezz	fez
fermentasion	fermentation	fezzant	pheasant
feromagnetic	ferromagnetic	fhonnagraf	phonograph
ferossity	ferocity	fiansay	fiancé or fiancée
ferral	feral	fibar	fiber
ferrett	ferret	fibberglas	fiberglass
ferrey	ferry	Fibbonacci	Fibonacci
ferrment	ferment	fibbralate	fibrillate
ferrocious	ferocious	fibbralation	fibrillation
ferrul	ferrule	fibbula	fibula
ferrus	ferrous	fibrossis	fibrosis
fertille	fertile	ficcsion	fiction
fertillity	fertility	fickal	fickle
fertillizer	fertilizer	ficticious	fictitious
fervant	fervent	fidd	fid
ferved	fervid	fiddel	fiddle
fesscue	fescue	fidellaty	fidelity
fesster	fester	fiducciery	fiduciary
festivel	festival	fiecuss	ficus
festivitty	festivity	fiesty	feisty
fether	feather	fiffe	fife

Incorrect	Correct	Incorrect	Correct
fifftieth	fiftieth	firey	fiery
figgmant	figment	firmamment	firmament
figgurine	figurine	firr tree	fir tree
figurrative	figurative	fischion	fission
figurratively	figuratively	fisherry	fishery
fillabuster	filibuster	fisscal	fiscal
fillagree	filigree	fisseur	fissure
fillament	filament	fissical	physical
fillanderer	philanderer	fistacuffs	fisticuffs
fillay	fillet	fistulla	fistula
fillbert	filbert	fite	fight
fillet menyon	filet mignon	fitfally	fitfully
filley	filly	fitfull	fitful
filliel	filial	fixxate	fixate
Fillipino	Filipino	fixxation	fixation
fillop	fillip	fizzel	fizzle
fillter	filter	flaak	flak
fillth	filth	flabbargast	flabbergast
fillthy	filthy	flac	flack
fin du seacle	fin de siècle	flacsid	flaccid
finelly	finally	flaer	flare
finerry	finery	flageolay	flageolet
fingerbord	fingerboard	flaggelate	flagellate
finnally	finale	flaggelum	flagellum
finnance	finance	flagrent	flagrant
finnancial	financial	flakey	flaky
finnancier	financier	flale	flail
finnangle	finagle	flamboyence	flamboyance
finneal	finial	flamboyent	flamboyant
finnese	finesse	flammenco	flamenco (dance)
finnicky	finicky		
finnite	finite	flammible	flammable
firbelow	furbelow	flammingo	flamingo (bird)

Incorrect	Correct	Incorrect	Correct
flanell	flannel	flexxtime	flextime
flannge	flange	fliar	flier
flashe	flash	flibbertyjibbet	flibbertigibbet
flasque	flask	flimsey	flimsy
flattary	flattery	flippency	flippancy
flattus	flatus	flite	flight
flatulant	flatulent	flixxer	flexor
flau	flaw	floc	flock
flaunder	flounder	flont	flaunt
flaur	flour	floo	flu
flauss	floss	floodgait	floodgate
flaut	flout	flooid	fluid
flauttest	flautist	flook	fluke
flauwer	flower	floom	flume
flaver	flavor	floorist	florist
flawd	flawed	flootist	flutist
flaxx	flax	florascope	fluoroscope
flayre	flair	floressence	fluorescence
fleace	fleece	floressent	fluorescent
flecher	fletcher	florest	florist
fledgeling	fledgling	florish	flourish
flegmattic	phlegmatic	florrid	florid
flei	flea	flotasion	flotation
flem	phlegm	flotsum	flotsam
flemflam	flimflam	flottila	flotilla
flench	flinch	flou	flue (air duct)
flent	flint	flounse	flounce
flentlock	flintlock	flowe	floe (ice)
flert	flirt	flowerry	flowery
flertation	flirtation	fluansy	fluency
flesch	flesh	fluant	fluent
flexable	flexible	fluccuate	fluctuate
flexx	flex	fluiddaty	fluidity

Incorrect	Correct	Incorrect	Correct
flunnky	flunky	forbiddan	forbidden
fluoradate	fluoridate	forboad	forebode
fluoressence	fluorescence	forboding	foreboding
flurroscope	fluoroscope	forcastle	forecastle
flusster	fluster	forcibally	forcibly
focuss	focus	forcibel	forcible
foddar	fodder	forcips	forceps
foel	foul	forclosure	foreclosure
foem	foam	forebad	forbade
foest	foist	forefit	forfeit
foibel	foible	forein	foreign
foke lore	folklore	forfinger	forefinger
fole	foal	forgerry	forgery
Folkner	Faulkner	forhand	forehand
follacle	follicle	forhead	forehead
follderol	folderol	forige	forage
folley	folly	forjery	forgery
folliation	foliation	forlorne	forlorn
folllge	foliage	formaldahide	formaldehyde
follio	folio	formallaty	formality
fome	foam	forman	foreman
fomment	foment	formasion	formation
fonagraf	phonograph	formatt	format
fondel	fondle	formel	formal
fondoo	fondue	formiddable	formidable
fonettic	phonetic	Formika	Formica
fonnic	phonic	formulla	formula
fontain	fountain	fornacate	fornicate
Foocauld	Foucault	forplay	foreplay
foogue	fugue	forray	foray
footahn	futon	forrensic	forensic
fopparry	foppery	forrest	forest
forbearence	forbearance	forrestry	forestry

Incorrect	Correct	Incorrect	Correct
forrge	forge	fractile	fractal
forrgo	forego	fracuss	fracas
forrth	fourth	fragill	fragile
forrum	forum	fragmenterry	fragmentary
forrunner	forerunner	fragrence	fragrance
forseen	foreseen	frai	fray
forshadow	foreshadow	frait	freight
forstall	forestall	frale	frail
fortafie	fortify	fraltee	frailty
fortatude	fortitude	Frances of Assissi	Francis of Assisi
fortay	forte	franchize	franchise
forteith	fortieth	frangibel	frangible
fortell	foretell	frangipanny	frangipani
forthrite	forthright	Frankanstine	Frankenstein
fortissamo	fortissimo	frankensense	frankincense
fortnite	fortnight	Fransiscan	Franciscan
fortrass	fortress	frantick	frantic
fortuitus	fortuitous	frappay	frappé
forword	foreword (book	fraternaty	fraternity
	introduction)	fraternel	fraternal
fosfurrus	phosphorus	fratraside	fratricide
fosille	fossil	frawd	fraud
foule	foil	frawdulant	fraudulent
foundasion	foundation	frawt	fraught
fountan	fountain	frazzel	frazzle
fourtine	fourteen	freckel	freckle
fourty	forty	freek	freak
fout	fought	freeky	freaky
fowle	fowl (bird)	freeley	freely
foyur	foyer	frenge	fringe
fraccious	fractious	frenzzy	frenzy
frachure	fracture	frequensy	frequency
fracsion	fraction	frequint	frequent

Incorrect	Correct	Incorrect	Correct
fressco	fresco	frozan	frozen
fretid	fretted	fruite	fruit
friare	friar	fruitfull	fruitful
friccassee	fricassee	fruittion	fruition
friccion	friction	frusterate	frustrate
friese	frieze	frustram	frustum
friet	fright	fryable	friable
friggate	frigate	fuall	fuel
Friggean	Phrygian	fude	feud
friggid	frigid	fujitive	fugitive
friggidity	frigidity	fullcram	fulcrum
frippary	frippery	fulley	fully
Frisby	Frisbee	fullfil	fulfill
friskee	frisky	full-fleged	full-fledged
frissahn	frisson	fullmanate	fulminate
fritatta	frittata	fullsome	fulsome
frite	fright	fumagant	fumigant
frivollaty	frivolity	fumbel	fumble
frivvalous	frivolous	fumeroll	fumarole
Froid	Freud	funcsion	function
Froidean	Freudian	functionerry	functionary
frolick	frolic	fundamentellist	fundamentalist
fronde	frond	funerrel	funeral (noun)
fronk	franc	funerrial	funereal (adjective)
frontaspiece	frontispiece		
fronteer	frontier	fung schway	feng shui
frontege	frontage	fungass	fungus
frontonn	fronton	fungicidde	fungicide
frooctose	fructose	funiculer	funicular
froo-froo	froufrou	funji	fungi
frotage	frottage	funjible	fungible
frothey	frothy	funnal	funnel
froun	frown	fureous	furious

Incorrect	Correct	Incorrect	Correct
furlow	furlough	fusallod	fusillade
furnature	furniture	fushea	fuchsia
furness	furnace	fusilage	fuselage
furra	furrow	fusile oil	fusel oil
furrbish	furbish	fussee	fusee
furror	furor (uproar)	futall	futile
furror	fuhrer (Ger. leader)	futillaty	futility
		futurizm	futurism
furrther	further	fuzel oil	fusel oil
furrtive	furtive	fuzion	fusion
furrze	furze	fuzzee	fusee

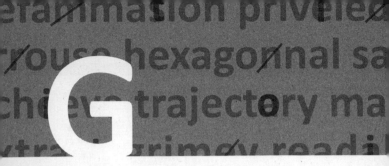

Most Commonly Misspelled Words

- gallant
- garbage
- ghastly
- giraffe
- gorgeous
- graduate
- grammar
- guarantee
- guidance
- guillotine

Incorrect	Correct	Incorrect	Correct
gabberdine	gabardine	galvannic	galvanic
gabel	gable	galvannize	galvanize
gaddabout	gadabout	gambal	gambol (leap, skip)
gaddfly	gadfly		
gadjit	gadget	gambel	gamble (bet)
gaege	gage (pledge)	gambet	gambit
gaege	gauge (measure)	gambrill	gambrel
Gaelick	Gaelic	gamma globbulen	gamma globulin
gaf	gaff (hook)	gammete	gamete
gaf	gaffe (error)	gammin	gamin
gail	gale	gammut	gamut
gaite	gait	gandar	gander
gaite	gate	gangleon	ganglion
galivant	gallivant	gangreene	gangrene
galla	gala	gannit	gannet
gallactic	galactic	gantlitt	gantlet
Gallahad	Galahad	gantree	gantry
Gallalean	Galilean	garbel	garble
Gallalee	Galilee	garbige	garbage
Gallaleo	Galileo	garbonzo	garbanzo
gallaria	galleria	gard	guard
gallary	gallery	gardennia	gardenia
gallax	galax	gargantuen	gargantuan
gallaxy	galaxy	gargel	gargle
gallen	gallon	gargoil	gargoyle
gallent	gallant	garlick	garlic
gallimaufrey	gallimaufry	garlicy	garlicky
gallion	galleon	garmet	garment
galloes	gallows	garnashee	garnishee
galloot	galoot	garnesh	garnish
gallopping	galloping	garnett	garnet
gallore	galore	garotte	garrote
gallupp	gallop	garrage	garage
gally	galley	garralous	garrulous

Incorrect	Correct	Incorrect	Correct
Garrimond	Garamond	geezar	geezer
garrish	garish	gefilta fish	gefilte fish
garrisson	garrison	geise	geese
garrit	garret	gelattinous	gelatinous
garson	garçon	gellaten	gelatin
gaskit	gasket	gellato	gelato
gassahol	gasohol	gellaty	gelati
gassious	gaseous	gellding	gelding
gassolene	gasoline	gellid	gelid
gasstly	ghastly	Gemani	Gemini
gastranommical	gastronomical	gendarm	gendarme
gastrick	gastric	geneology	genealogy
gastroenterrology	gastroenterology	geeneous	genius
gastroentestinnal	gastrointestinal	geenus	genus
Gattling gun	Gatling gun	generossity	generosity
gauk	gawk	generus	generous
gauntlit	gauntlet	geney	genie
gause	gauze	Gengiss Khan	Genghis Khan
gavvel	gavel	gennasis	genesis
gavvot	gavotte	gennative	genitive
gawdy	gaudy	gennder	gender
gayaty	gaiety	genneral	general
gaylax	galax	genneralization	generalization
gaylaxy	galaxy	gennerate	generate
gaysha	geisha	gennerator	generator
gazpaccio	gazpacho	genneric	generic
Gazza	Gaza	gennetics	genetics
gazzateer	gazetteer	gennial	genial
gazzeebo	gazebo	gennocide	genocide
gazzele	gazelle	gennotype	genotype
gazzet	gazette	gennuflect	genuflect
geak	geek	gennuine	genuine
gecco	gecko	genous	genius
geenome	genome	genruh	genre

Incorrect	Correct	Incorrect	Correct
genteele	genteel	Gethsemminy	Gethsemane
gentel	gentle	getto	ghetto
gentriffy	gentrify	Gewurstraminner	Gewurztraminer
genuflexion	genuflection	Ghanna	Ghana
genyus	genius	ghelding	gelding
geocentrick	geocentric	ghoolish	ghoulish
geodde	geode	ghostley	ghostly
geodesick	geodesic	ghout	gout
geollogy	geology	gibben	gibbon
geommatry	geometry	gibblit	giblet
geommetric	geometric	gibbuss	gibbous
geophissics	geophysics	Gibralter	Gibraltar
geostationery	geostationary	gigantick	gigantic
gerbal	gerbil	giggahurtz	gigahertz
gerd	gird	giggolo	gigolo
gerdel	girdle	gimbel	gimbal
gerder	girder	gimlitt	gimlet
gerkin	gherkin	gimmeck	gimmick
germain	germane	gimmpy	gimpy
germanate	germinate	ginghem	gingham
germmacide	germicide	gingir	ginger
gerontollogy	gerontology	ginko	ginkgo
gerranium	geranium	ginsing	ginseng
gerrontocracy	gerontocracy	gippsy	gypsy
gerrund	gerund	girraffe	giraffe
gerryatric	geriatric	gisst	gist
gerrymandar	gerrymander	gizzerd	gizzard
gerth	girth	gizzmo	gizmo
gesoondhite	gesundheit	glabruss	glabrous
gesst	guest	glaceir	glacier
gestacion	gestation	glaciel	glacial
gesticullate	gesticulate	gladiatter	gladiator
Gestoppo	Gestapo	gladiolla	gladiola
gestuer	gesture	glaire	glare

Incorrect	Correct	Incorrect	Correct
glammorous	glamorous	gobblin	goblin
glanduller	glandular	Goddiva	Godiva
glaucomma	glaucoma	gode	goad
gleem	gleam	godess	goddess
gleen	glean	Godforsakin	Godforsaken
glent	glint	goffer	gofer
glibb	glib	gogles	goggles
glidder	glider	goitter	goiter
glimmar	glimmer	Goldalocks	Goldilocks
glimse	glimpse	gole	goal
glisando	glissando	Golieth	Goliath
gloamming	gloaming	golum	golem
globbular	globular	Gommorah	Gomorrah
globel	global	gondala	gondola
globely	globally	gondalier	gondolier
glockenspeil	glockenspiel	Gondhi	Gandhi
gloo	glue	gonnad	gonad
glorrify	glorify	gonnarea	gonorrhea
glossery	glossary	Gooda cheese	Gouda cheese
glossey	glossy	googloplex	googolplex
glossolallia	glossolalia	goolog	gulag
glote	gloat	goolosh	goulash
glowwer	glower	goord	gourd
gluclose	glucose	Gordean knot	Gordian knot
glutan	gluten	gordge	gorge
glutius	gluteus	gorgan	gorgon
glutten	glutton	gorgious	gorgeous
gluttiny	gluttony	gorrilla	gorilla (ape)
gniece	gneiss	goshe	gauche
gnoem	gnome	gospil	gospel
gnoman	gnomon	gossammer	gossamer
Gnosstic	Gnostic	gossup	gossip
goattee	goatee	gote	goat
gobblet	goblet	gotthic	gothic

Incorrect	Correct	Incorrect	Correct
gouash	gouache	grappel	grapple
gouje	gouge	grappnel	grapnel
goul	ghoul	grassp	grasp
govennor	governor	grattafication	gratification
governence	governance	gratte	grate (shred, like cheese)
govvern	govern		
grabbel	grabble	gratte	great (super)
graceous	gracious	grattitude	gratitude
gradduate	graduate	gratto	grotto
gradiant	gradient	grattuatous	gratuitous
graduasion	graduation	grattuaty	gratuity
graduel	gradual	graut	grout
graffite	graphite	gravally	gravelly
graffitti	graffiti	gravamin	gravamen
grakkel	grackle	gravelly	gravely
gramace	grimace	gravetis	gravitas
grammaphone	gramophone	gravin	graven
grammattical	grammatical	gravvel	gravel
grammer	grammar	gravvid	gravid
grammerian	grammarian	gravvitate	gravitate
grampass	grampus	gravvity	gravity
gran moll	grand mal	grayhounde	greyhound
gran pree	grand prix	grayl	grail
grandeose	grandiose	greate	grate (shred, like cheese)
grandilloquent	grandiloquent		
grane	grain	greate	great (wonderful)
granje	grange	greatfull	grateful
granjure	grandeur	greeb	grebe
grannary	granary	greef	grief
grannite	granite	greenbryar	greenbrier
grannulated	granulated	greengo	gringo
grannuler	granular	Greenich	Greenwich
grapheem	grapheme	greenry	greenery
graphollagy	graphology	greese	grease

Incorrect	Correct	Incorrect	Correct
greesy	greasy	growtesk	grotesque
greevance	grievance	grubily	grubbily
gregarrious	gregarious	grudje	grudge
Gregorrean	Gregorian	gruil	gruel
gremlen	gremlin	grumbily	grumbly
Grendal	Grendel	grundge	grunge
grennade	grenade	grundgy	grungy
grennadier	grenadier	grunnion	grunion
grennadine	grenadine	guaccamole	guacamole
Greshem's law	Gresham's law	guacho	gaucho
grewsome	gruesome	guage	gauge
griddel	griddle	guant	gaunt
gridirron	gridiron	Guantannamo	Guantanamo
griepp	grippe	guardean	guardian
grievuss	grievous	guarden	garden
grimey	grimy	Guarnareus	Guarnerius
grimme	grim	guarrantee	guarantee
grimmis	grimace	Guattamalla	Guatemala
grissle	gristle	guavva	guava
grissly	grisly	gubbernatorial	gubernatorial
grizzel	grizzle	guber	goober
groap	grope	gudginn	gudgeon
grocerry	grocery	gueld	guild
groen	groin	guelt	guilt
grograin	grosgrain	guerilla	guerrilla (fighter)
grommit	grommet	Guernsy	Guernsey
grone	groan	guesst	guessed
groop	group	guffah	guffaw
grouce	grouse	guidence	guidance
grouchey	grouchy	guideon	guidon
groul	growl	guilde	gild
groundbraking	groundbreaking	guillatine	guillotine
groupper	grouper	guille	guile
grovvel	grovel	guilte	gilt

Incorrect	Correct	Incorrect	Correct
guinny	guinea	Guttanberg	Gutenberg
guittar	guitar	guttarel	guttural
gullable	gullible	guyse	guise
gullit	gullet	guyser	geyser
gumpsion	gumption	gwano	guano
gunnal	gunnel	gyanandrus	gynandrous
gunnell	gunwale	gymnaseum	gymnasium
gunneysac	gunnysack	gymnasticks	gymnastics
gurken	gherkin	gymnist	gymnast
gurny	gurney	gynacollogy	gynecology
gurrmay	gourmet	gypsem	gypsum
gurrmond	gourmand	gyrascope	gyroscope
gurrue	guru	gyrfalkan	gyrfalcon or gerfalcon
gussit	gusset		
gustalt	gestalt	gyrocumpass	gyrocompass
gustatorry	gustatory	gyrrate	gyrate
gutta purtcha	gutta-percha		

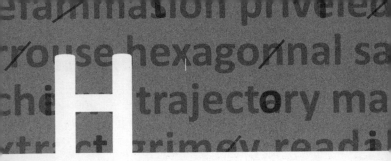

Most Commonly Misspelled Words

- hallelujah
- handful
- handkerchief
- hesitate
- hiccup
- hieroglyphics
- holiday
- honest
- hors d'oeuvres
- humorous

Incorrect	Correct	Incorrect	Correct
habachi	hibachi	hallogin	halogen
habbatat	habitat	hallucinnogen	hallucinogen
habberdasher	haberdasher	hallusannate	hallucinate
habbichual	habitual	haloe	halo
habbitable	habitable	halsyon	halcyon
habbitant	habitant	haltar	halter
habbituate	habituate	halyerd	halyard or haliard
habillament	habiliment		
habillatate	habilitate	hamlitt	hamlet
habittuay	habitué	hammadriad	hamadryad
habius corpus	habeas corpus	hammar	hammer
hackcls	hackles	hammate bone	hamate bone
hackneed	hackneyed	hammster	hamster
hackny	hackney	hammstring	hamstring
haddoc	haddock	hammuck	hammock
Hadrean's wall	Hadrian's wall	hancho	honcho
hael	hale (healthy)	handfull	handful
haggerd	haggard	handsome cab	hansom cab
haggiology	hagiology	handycap	handicap
hagiss	haggis	handycraft	handicraft
haikoo	haiku	handywork	handiwork
hair-brained	hare-brained	hangor	hangar (for planes or hanger (for clothes)
hairem	harem		
hairlip	harelip		
Haishean	Haitian		
Halell	Hallel	hankerchief	handkerchief
halestone	hailstone	hankey-pankey	hanky-panky
half nellson	half nelson	Hannaka	Hanukkah or Hannukah
Halie's comet	Halley's comet		
hallaluya	hallelujah	hannger	hangar (for planes or hanger (for clothes)
hallapanyo	jalapeño		
hallibut	halibut		
halloe	hallow	hansome	handsome
Halloeen	Halloween	haphazzerd	haphazard

Incorrect	Correct	Incorrect	Correct
happanstants	happenstance	hassenfeffer	hasenpfeffer
hapployd	haploid	hassienda	hacienda
harbenger	harbinger	hasta luewago	hasta luego
harc	hark	hatchett	hatchet
hardpann	hardpan	hatefull	hateful
hardwear	hardware	hatrid	hatred
harken	hearken	hauk	hawk
harlet	harlot	haund	hound
harleyquin	harlequin	haur	hour
harmoneous	harmonious	hauthorn	hawthorn
harmonnic	harmonic	Hauthorn effect	Hawthorne effect
harmonnica	harmonica	hautty	haughty
harmonnize	harmonize	hauzer	hawser
harniss	harness	havan	haven
harpest	harpist	havvarty	havarti
harpoone	harpoon	havversac	haversack
harpsacord	harpsichord	havvock	havoc
harraden	harridan	Hawaiya	Hawaii
harrang	harangue	Hawaiyan	Hawaiian
harrasment	harassment	hawnt	haunt
harrear	harrier	hayday	heyday
Harri Krishna	Hare Krishna	Haydez	Hades
harrico	haricot	haynous	heinous
harri-karri	hara-kiri	hazell	hazel
harro	harrow	hazzard	hazard
harrumf	harrumph	hazzardus	hazardous
harsch	harsh	headake	headache
hartebeast	hartebeest	headress	headdress
harth	hearth	heaft	heft
hartthrob	heartthrob	heale	heal (cure) or heel (foot)
harvist	harvest		
hasheesh	hashish	heall	heal (cure) or heel (foot)
hassac	hassock		
hassel	hassle	healthfull	healthful

Incorrect	Correct	Incorrect	Correct
heartilly	heartily	hellicopter	helicopter
heavilly	heavily	hellmet	helmet
heavvier	heavier	hellotry	helotry
heckell	heckle	hellyon	hellion
hectogram	hectogram	hemm	hymn
hectarring	hectoring	hemmacrania	hemicrania
hecter	hectare	hemmademmasemmaquaver	
hectick	hectic		hemidemisemiquaver
heddel	heddle	hemmaglobin	hemoglobin
hedonnism	hedonism	hemmaphilia	hemophilia
heedlass	heedless	hemmaplegic	hemiplegic
heeth	heath	hemmaroid	hemorrhoid
heethen	heathen	hemmasfere	hemisphere
heether	heather	hemmatology	hematology
heeve	heave	hemmloc	hemlock
heffer	heifer	hemmorige	hemorrhage
heffty	hefty	henbain	henbane
hege	hedge	Hendi	Hindi
hegemmony	hegemony	henge	hinge
heirarchy	hierarchy	hennah	henna
heiroglyphics	hieroglyphics	henseforth	henceforth
hejirra	hejira or hegira	henshman	henchman
hela monster	Gila monster	henterland	hinterland
helascious	hellacious	heppatitis	hepatitis
heleum	helium	heptigon	heptagon
helgremmite	hellgrammite	herassy	heresy
heliatrope	heliotrope	heratick	heretic
helickel	helical	herbacide	herbicide
helics	helix	herbacious	herbaceous
hellabore	hellebore	herbel	herbal
Hellaspont	Hellespont	herbivvarus	herbivorous
Hellenick	Hellenic	Hercullean	Herculean
helleocentric	heliocentric	herediterry	hereditary
hellical	helical	herematige	hermitage

Incorrect	Correct	Incorrect	Correct
hermafrodite	hermaphrodite	hickup	hiccup
hermanootics	hermeneutics	hiddeous	hideous
hermettic	hermetic	hidraullic	hydraulic
hermitt	hermit	hidrosus	hydrosis
hernea	hernia	hieghth	height
herpees	herpes	hier	heir
herrald	herald	hierling	hireling
herras	harass	hierloom	heirloom
Herrcales	Hercules	hiest	heist
herredity	heredity	hiett	height
herreldry	heraldry	higeen	hygiene
herrengbone	herringbone	highfallutin	highfalutin
herritage	heritage	highjac	hijack
herriticle	heretical	highten	heighten
herroic	heroic	hikoo	haiku
herroine	heroine	hillarity	hilarity
herron	heron	hillarreous	hilarious
herse	hearse	hilluck	hillock
hersuit	hirsute	Himelick	Heimlich
hessatate	hesitate	himen	hymen
hessitent	hesitant	himenoptera	Hymenoptera
hetterodoxy	heterodoxy	himm	hymn
hetterogenious	heterogeneous	Himmalayas	Himalayas
hetterosexual	heterosexual	himp	hemp
hevvenly	heavenly	hindar	hinder
hexadessammal	hexadecimal	hindrence	hindrance
hexagonnal	hexagonal	hipadermic	hypodermic
heyfield	hayfield	hiperbollic	hyperbolic
hi alie	jai alai	hiperopia	hyperopia
hiattas	hiatus	hipnatise	hypnotize
hiattel	hiatal	hipnosis	hypnosis
hibarnate	hibernate	hippacampus	hippocampus
hibiscuss	hibiscus	hippapottamus	hippopotamus
hickerry	hickory	Hippocratees	Hippocrates

Incorrect	Correct	Incorrect	Correct
hippodroam	hippodrome	homested	homestead
hippster	hipster	homiopathic	homeopathic
hirsuit	hirsute	hommage	homage
Hispannic	Hispanic	hommanid	hominid
histamene	histamine	hommanoid	hominoid
historrean	historian	hommiletic	homiletic
historrical	historical	hommily	homily
histrionnics	histrionics	hommonoid	homonoid
hi-tek	high-tech	hommonym	homonym
hoagey	hoagie	hommophobia	homophobia
hoan	hone	homo sapians	homo sapiens
hoarde	hoard	homocidal	homicidal
hoare	hoar (gray, frost)	homoerrotic	homoerotic
hobbel	hobble	homogenious	homogeneous
hobgobblin	hobgoblin	homogennize	homogenize
Hobsen's choice	Hobson's choice	homosexuallity	homosexuality
hocky	hockey	homosexuel	homosexual
hodgepodge	hodgepodge	homuncullus	homunculus
hodown	hoedown	honch	haunch
hoerse	hoarse	honeysuccle	honeysuckle
Hogmannay	Hogmanay	honkee-tonk	honky-tonk
hoitty-toitty	hoity-toity	honner	honor
hokes	hoax	honnest	honest
hokus-pokus	hocus-pocus	Honnika	Hanukkah
hollendaise	hollandaise	honnor	honor
holliday	holiday	honnorable	honorable
hollihauk	hollyhock	honnorerium	honorarium
hollistic	holistic	honnorery	honorary
Hollocost	Holocaust	honoriffic	honorific
hollograph	holograph	hoodlem	hoodlum
Holsteen	Holstein	hookuh	hookah
holyness	holiness	hoola	hula
homberg	homburg	hoolagan	hooligan
hombray	hombre	hoonta	junta

Incorrect	Correct	Incorrect	Correct
hooping cough	whooping cough	hostiss	hostess
hootanannie	hootenanny	hostuh	hosta (plant)
Hoozier	Hoosier	hote coture	haute couture
hopefull	hopeful	hote cuizine	haute cuisine
Hopey	Hopi	hotellier	hotelier
hopscoch	hopscotch	Hottantot	Hottentot
hor d'urve	hors d'oeuvres	houl	howl
hord	horde (crowd)	housefraw	hausfrau
hord	hoard (save)	houzing	housing
horehouse	whorehouse	hovvel	hovel
horhound	horehound	howitzar	howitzer
hormoan	hormone	howley	haole
hornit	hornet	hoy polloy	hoi polloi
horrable	horrible	hoyst	hoist
horrascope	horoscope	hozannah	hosanna
horred	horrid	hu	hue
horrendus	horrendous	Hubbell	Hubble
horrer	horror	hubriss	hubris
horrizon	horizon	huckelberry	huckleberry
horrizontal	horizontal	huckstir	huckster
horsepowwer	horsepower	huddel	huddle
horsreddish	horseradish	hueristic	heuristic
hortaculture	horticulture	Hugonot	Huguenot
hortatorry	hortatory	huhbub	hubbub
hoserry	hosiery	hullaballoo	hullabaloo
hospis	hospice	humain	humane
hospitallity	hospitality	humanitarrian	humanitarian
hospittable	hospitable	humannoid	humanoid
hospittal	hospital	humas	humus
hosslar	hostler	humbel	humble
hostellery	hostelry	humectent	humectant
hostige	hostage	humer	humor
hostill	hostile	humeresque	humoresque
hostillaty	hostility	humeris	humerus (bone)

Incorrect	Correct	Incorrect	Correct
humeris	humorous (funny)	hydrollagist	hydrologist
		hydrollagy	hydrology
humerous	humerus (bone)	hydrollasis	hydrolysis
humerous	humorous (funny)	hydrommater	hydrometer
		hydroxxide	hydroxide
humidatty	humidity	hyenna	hyena
humilleation	humiliation	hygeine	hygiene
humilliate	humiliate	hygenic	hygienic
hummanist	humanist	hymnel	hymnal
hummas	hummus	hypadermic	hypodermic
hummuck	hummock	hyperbalee	hyperbole
hummunculous	homunculus	hyperbolla	hyperbola
huncker	hunker	hyperbollic	hyperbolic
hundridth	hundredth	hyperropia	hyperopia
hurdel	hurdle (barrier)	hypertencion	hypertension
hurdle	hurtle (hurl)	hyperthiroidism	hyperthyroidism
hurracane	hurricane	hypertraffy	hypertrophy
hurtz	hertz	hyperventillation	hyperventilation
huskey	husky	hypnatise	hypnotize
hussel	hustle	hypnossis	hypnosis
husser	hussar	hypnottic	hypnotic
hustengs	hustings	hypochrondea	hypochondria
huvver	hover	hypochrondeac	hypochondriac
Hwuinnim	Houyhnhnm	hypocrissy	hypocrisy
hyasinth	hyacinth	hypocritt	hypocrite
hybred	hybrid	hypothallamus	hypothalamus
hydrangia	hydrangea	hypothassis	hypothesis
hydraphobea	hydrophobia	hypothermea	hypothermia
hydrawlic	hydraulic	hypottenuse	hypotenuse
hydrocephallus	hydrocephalus	hysterea	hysteria
hydrodynammic	hydrodynamic	hysterectamy	hysterectomy
hydrogin	hydrogen		

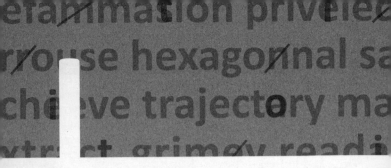

Most Commonly Misspelled Words

- imaginary
- immediately
- inalienable
- incidentally
- interference
- interruption
- inconsequential
- irrelevant
- irritable
- itchy

Incorrect	Correct	Incorrect	Correct
I Cheng	I Ching	idiapathic	idiopathic
iambick	iambic	idiolec	idiolect
ibbex	ibex	idiology	ideology
ibbis	ibis	idiot savvant	idiot savant
I-beem	I-beam	idolen	eidolon
Iberrean	Iberian	idoll	idle (not working)
ibuproffin	ibuprofen		
Icarean	Icarian	idoll	idol (admired one)
ichy	itchy		
Ickarus	Icarus	idollatrous	idolatrous
icktheology	ichthyology	idylic	idyllic
iconn	icon	igglue	igloo
iconnoclast	iconoclast	ignious	igneous
iconoklastic	iconoclastic	ignission	ignition
icycle	icicle	ignobel	ignoble
icyly	icily	ignominneous	ignominious
iday feecs	idée fixe	ignommany	ignominy
iddiamatic	idiomatic	ignorramus	ignoramus
iddiosincracy	idiosyncrasy	ignorrence	ignorance
iddiosincrattic	idiosyncratic	ignorrent	ignorant
iddiot	idiot	igwanna	iguana
iddium	idiom	ilck	ilk
ideagram	ideogram	Illead	Iliad
ideelism	idealism	illeggible	illegible
ideelistic	idealistic	illegittimate	illegitimate
idel	idle (not working)	illegle	illegal
		illeum	ileum
idel	idol (admired one)	illimmitible	illimitable
		illiteration	alliteration
identacle	identical	illitterite	illiterate
identaty	identity	illium	ilium
ideolog	ideologue	illuseon	illusion
ider	eider	illustreous	illustrious
idettic	eidetic	imatereal	immaterial

Incorrect	Correct	Incorrect	Correct
imballance	imbalance	impathy	empathy
imbasellic	imbecilic	impatiant	impatient
imbasill	imbecile	impatigo	impetigo
imbellish	embellish	impations	impatiens (flower)
imbibbe	imbibe		
imboss	emboss	impattense	impotence
imboue	imbue	impatus	impetus
imbrio	embryo	impeccunious	impecunious
imbroil	embroil	impeckible	impeccable
imemmorial	immemorial	impeddament	impediment
imemorial	immemorial	impeed	impede
immaccullate	immaculate	impell	impel
immaginare	imaginary	impellar	impeller
immago	imago	impenge	impinge
immalashun	immolation	impennatrable	impenetrable
immatereal	immaterial	impeous	impious
immateur	immature	imperfecsion	imperfection
immeasureable	immeasurable	impermeabel	impermeable
Immediatley	immediately	imperrative	imperative
immegrate	immigrate (move into)	imperreal	imperial
		imperril	imperil
immerce	immerse	imperseptible	imperceptible
immercion	immersion	impersonnate	impersonate
immessurably	immeasurably	impertenance	impertinence
immobilise	immobilize	imperterbible	imperturbable
immoliant	emollient	impettuous	impetuous
immovabel	immovable	impiaty	impiety
immpale	impale	implacate	implicate
immunisation	immunization	implaccable	implacable
immutible	immutable	implament	implement
impass	impasse	implissit	implicit
impassibel	impassable	impload	implode
impatense	impotence	imployee	employee

Incorrect	Correct	Incorrect	Correct
impondarible	imponderable	in memmoriem	in memoriam
impoote	impute	in utarro	in utero
importence	importance	inaccesable	inaccessible
importoon	importune	inaddaquacy	inadequacy
impossition	imposition	inadvirtant	inadvertent
imposstor	imposter	inaleanible	inalienable
impoverrish	impoverish	inamored	enamored
impoze	impose	inate	innate
impractacable	impracticable	inauddable	inaudible
impragnate	impregnate	Incah	Inca
impragnible	impregnable	incalcullable	incalculable
impramature	imprimatur	incandessant	incandescent
impresionism	impressionism	incannabula	incunabula
impressario	impresario	incannoe	inconnu
impresst	imprest (funds)	incantasion	incantation
improbbable	improbable	incappassitate	incapacitate
impropriaty	impropriety	incarnet	incarnate
improptu	impromptu	incarserrate	incarcerate
improvize	improvise	incennarate	incinerate
improvvadint	improvident	incessent	incessant
imprudant	imprudent	inciddant	incident
impudanse	impudence	incidently	incidentally
impudunt	impudent	incindiarry	incendiary
impulce	impulse	incippiant	incipient
impullsive	impulsive	inciscion	incision
impunatty	impunity	inciscive	incisive
impune	impugn	inclimment	inclement
impurrity	impurity	inclinnation	inclination
impurtune	importune	inclusseon	inclusion
impurveous	impervious	incogneto	incognito
imune	immune	incoherrant	incoherent
imunity	immunity	incoit	inchoate
in absintea	in absentia	incommunacative	incommunicative

Incorrect	Correct	Incorrect	Correct
incomodeous	incommodious	indafattagable	indefatigable
incomparrable	incomparable	indagense	indigence
incompatable	incompatible	indagestion	indigestion
incompatant	incompetent	indago	indigo
incomprehensable		indeccarous	indecorous
	incomprehensible	indecipherible	indecipherable
inconcievable	inconceivable	indecissive	indecisive
inconcloosive	inconclusive	indeffinite	indefinite
incongarrous	incongruous	indellable	indelible
incongruant	incongruent	indellacasy	indelicacy
inconsaquential	inconsequential	indemnafy	indemnify
inconsistant	inconsistent	indensure	indenture
inconsolible	inconsolable	independance	independence
Inconspiccuous	inconspicuous	indesancy	indecency
incontinnent	incontinent	indescribabel	indescribable
inconvenniant	inconvenient	indetermannit	indeterminate
incorporrial	incorporeal	indettedness	indebtedness
incorragible	incorrigible	indiccative	indicative
incorruptable	incorruplible	indifferanse	indifference
increddible	incredible	indiginous	indigenous
increddulaty	incredulity	indignent	indignant
incredulus	incredulous	indimnafy	indemnify
incremment	increment	indiscresion	indiscretion
incrimminate	incriminate	indiscrimmanately	indiscriminately
incrypt	encrypt	indispinsible	indispensable
incubasion	incubation	indistinguishible	indistinguishable
incubuss	incubus	indite	indict
incullcate	inculcate	indivizable	indivisible
incumbansy	incumbency	indivvidualism	individualism
incurcion	incursion	indolance	indolence
incureous	incurious	indolant	indolent
incurrable	incurable	indomorf	endomorph
indaccation	indication	inndorse	endorse

Incorrect	Correct	Incorrect	Correct
indubatibly	indubitably	inflexable	inflexible
induccsion	induction	inflimmation	inflammation
indullgense	indulgence	influanse	influence
indullgent	indulgent	influencial	influential
industreal	industrial	influinza	influenza
ineddible	inedible	influxx	influx
ineffible	ineffable	informent	informant
inelligible	ineligible	infraccion	infraction
inershia	inertia	infrenge	infringe
inestimmable	inestimable	infrustructure	infrastructure
inevittable	inevitable	infuryate	infuriate
inexorrable	inexorable	infusian	infusion
inexpliccable	inexplicable	ingraciating	ingratiating
infallable	infallible	ingraditude	ingratitude
infammy	infamy	ingrashiate	ingratiate
infantaside	infanticide	ingreat	ingrate
infante terrribel	enfant terrible	ingreediant	ingredient
infarcsion	infarction	ingres	ingress
infattuated	infatuated	ingross	engross
infeasable	infeasible	inguinnel	inguinal
infeccious	infectious	ingut	ingot
infeebled	enfeebled	inhabbatent	inhabitant
infered	inferred	inhabition	inhibition
inferrance	inference	inhance	enhance
inferrno	inferno	inherant	inherent
infidellaty	infidelity	inherratance	inheritance
infilltrate	infiltrate	inhumannity	inhumanity
infinnatesimal	infinitesimal	inimmical	inimical
infinnative	infinitive	iniquitty	iniquity
infirmery	infirmary	inishative	initiative
inflamible	inflammable	injeck	inject
inflationery	inflationary	injenious	ingenious
infleccion	inflection	injenuous	ingenuous

Incorrect	Correct	Incorrect	Correct
injest	ingest	inquizision	inquisition
injureous	injurious	insaciable	insatiable
inkwest	inquest	insannity	insanity
inmatty	enmity	insciser	incisor
innane	inane	insconse	ensconce
innapropriate	inappropriate	inscrutible	inscrutable
innapt	inapt	insectavore	insectivore
innarticulit	inarticulate	insemmination	insemination
innaugural	inaugural	insense	incense
innauspiciously	inauspiciously	insensittive	insensitive
innead	ennead	insentiv	incentive
innebreate	inebriate	insepperable	inseparable
inneluctible	ineluctable	inseption	inception
innept	incpt	insestuous	incestuous
innercept	intercept	inshrine	enshrine
Innercoastal Waterway		insiddious	insidious
	Intracoastal Waterway	insiggnea	insignia
innerdenominational		insigniffacant	insignificant
	interdenominational	insinnuate	insinuate
innerdict	interdict	insipped	insipid
innerlude	interlude	insistance	insistence
innernecine	internecine	insistant	insistent
innert	inert	inslave	enslave
inngrave	engrave	insollance	insolence
innocense	innocence	insolluble	insoluble
innoculate	inoculate	insomnea	insomnia
innumerrabel	innumerable	insousiance	insouciance
innundate	inundate	insparation	inspiration
innure	inure	inspecter	inspector
inoccuous	innocuous	instabillaty	instability
inordennate	inordinate	instagate	instigate
inovation	innovation	instantannious	instantaneous
inquisittive	inquisitive	insted	instead

Incorrect	Correct	Incorrect	Correct
instence	instance	intermetzo	intermezzo
institutionnal	institutional	interminnable	interminable
instruccion	instruction	intermittant	intermittent
instrummental	instrumental	internellize	internalize
insubordinnation	insubordination	interoggatory	interrogatory
insue	ensue	interplannitary	interplanetary
insufficiant	insufficient	Interpoll	Interpol
insulan	insulin	interpollate	interpolate
insulater	insulator	interprit	interpret
insuler	insular	interragation	interrogation
insullation	insulation	interragator	interrogator
insurection	insurrection	interrim	interim
insurence	insurance	intersede	intercede
insurgince	insurgence	interspurse	intersperse
insurgints	insurgents	intersticial	interstitial
intallio	intaglio	interuption	interruption
intamacy	intimacy	interveen	intervene
intangibel	intangible	intervel	interval
integraty	integrity	intesstate	intestate
integrel	integral	intigrate	integrate
intelectual	intellectual	intijer	integer
intelligencia	intelligentsia	intimmadate	intimidate
intensafy	intensify	intollerence	intolerance
intensional	intentional	intollerent	intolerant
intercesion	intercession	intonnation	intonation
interdisciplinery	interdisciplinary	intooitive	intuitive
interegnam	interregnum	intoxxicate	intoxicate
interferranse	interference	intracate	intricate
interferron	interferon	intractible	intractable
interjeccion	interjection	intraducsion	introduction
interloccuter	interlocutor	intramurrel	intramural
interlopper	interloper	intransagint	intransigent
intermediery	intermediary	intransative	intransitive

Incorrect	Correct	Incorrect	Correct
intraspecion	introspection	inviddious	invidious
intrauterrin	intrauterine	inviggerate	invigorate
intravanous	intravenous	invizion	envision
intravirt	introvert	invollentary	involuntary
intreeg	intrigue	invullnerable	invulnerable
intrench	entrench	iodised	iodized
intrensic	intrinsic	ionnasphere	ionosphere
intreppid	intrepid	Ionnian	Ionian
introet	introit	ionnize	ionize
introod	intrude	iottacism	iotacism
introoder	intruder	ippecack	ipecac
introverseon	introversion	ippso facto	ipso facto
intruseon	intrusion	ircksome	irksome
intuission	intuition	iregular	irregular
inuendo	innuendo	iriss	iris
Inuett	Inuit or Innuit	irmin	ermine
invacation	invocation	irradeate	irradiate
invagenate	invaginate	irradescent	iridescent
invagle	inveigle	Irranian	Iranian
invallid	invalid	Irraquoy	Iroquois
invaluble	invaluable	irrascible	irascible
invarriably	invariably	irrassional	irrational
invay	inveigh	irratable	irritable
invazion	invasion	irreconsilable	irreconcilable
invazive	invasive	irredemable	irredeemable
invectave	invective	irrefutible	irrefutable
inventorry	inventory	irreligeous	irreligious
invertabrate	invertebrate	irrellavent	irrelevant
inverzion	inversion	irreparrible	irreparable
investagation	investigation	irrepressable	irrepressible
investigattor	investigator	irreproachible	irreproachable
invetterate	inveterate	irresalute	irresolute
invialable	inviolable	irresonsable	irresponsible

Incorrect	Correct	Incorrect	Correct
irrevocabel	irrevocable	Isslam	Islam
irrevvarent	irreverent	issmus	isthmus
irridectamy	iridectomy	issobar	isobar
irritasion	irritation	issuence	issuance
irronic	ironic	itallacise	italicize
isathurm	isotherm	itallic	italic
isatonnic	isotonic	itennerary	itinerary
isatope	isotope	itinnerent	itinerant
isossales	isosceles	itterate	iterate
issalation	isolation	itts	its (possessive), or it's (it is)
issametric	isometric		
issinglass	isinglass	ivary	ivory

J & K

Most Commonly Misspelled Words

- jacuzzi
- jealousy
- jeopardy
- jewelry
- judgment
- juvenile
- ketchup
- kindergarten
- koala
- knowledge

Incorrect	Correct	Incorrect	Correct
Jabbarwokky	Jabberwocky	jellatin	gelatin
jabbor	jabber	jellato	gelato
jaccarnada	jacaranda	jellid	gelid
Jaccobin	Jacobin	jellous	jealous
jaccuzi	jacuzzi	jender	gender
jackalantern	jack-o'-lantern	Jengiss Kon	Genghis Khan
jackel	jackal	jenneology	genealogy
jackenapes	jackanapes	jennerosity	generosity
jacknife	jackknife	jennerous	generous
jactatatin	jactitation	jenney	jenny
jagguar	jaguar	jentile	gentile
joi olie	jai alai	jenuine	genuine
jajune	jejune	jepperdize	jeopardize
jallapanyo	jalapeño	jepperdy	jeopardy
jallasie	jalousie (blinds)	jerbil	gerbil
jallasie	jealousy (feeling of resentment)	jerfalcon	gyrfalcon
		jeriatrick	geriatric
jambe	jamb	jerraboem	jeroboam
jambellaya	jambalaya	jerramiad	jeremiad
jamborree	jamboree	jerrund	gerund
jangel	jangle	jerry-bilt	jerry-built
janittor	janitor	jerrymander	gerrymander
jannitoreal	janitorial	jestalt	gestalt
Jannus	Janus	jestate	gestate
janrah	genre	jestation	gestation
Januerry	January	jesticulllate	gesticulate
jargun	jargon	jestor	jester
jaspar	jasper	jesture	gesture
javvalin	javelin	jetsem	jetsam
jawndice	jaundice	jettason	jettison
jawnt	jaunt	jewellary	jewelry
Jaynus	Janus	jeweller	jeweler
jazzmin	jasmine	jezzabel	jezebel
Jekell and Hide	Jekyll and Hyde	Jezzuit	Jesuit

Incorrect	Correct	Incorrect	Correct
Jezzuittical	Jesuitical	judgemint	judgment
jibberish	gibberish	judiscial	judicial
jibbet	gibbet	judiscierry	judiciary
jiblit	giblet	judiscious	judicious
jiggalo	gigolo	jue nu say quoa	je ne sais quoi
jihodd	jihad	juggarnaut	juggernaut
jinger	ginger	jugguler	jugular
jingoizm	jingoism	jujittsy	jujitsu
jirate	gyrate	jujubbe	jujube
jittney	jitney	julipp	julep
joccularrity	jocularity	Julliard	Juilliard
jocculer	jocular	julyann	julienne
joccund	jocund	junapper	juniper
jocky	jockey	junchure	juncture
jodpurrs	jodhpurs	jungel	jungle
joecose	jocose	junkit	junket
Joeharry	Johari	junko	junco
joeist	joist	jurisprudense	jurisprudence
johnquill	jonquil	jurnal	journal
jondarm	gendarme	jurnalism	journalism
jonnboat	johnboat	jurnalist	journalist
joonta	junta	jurrasdiction	jurisdiction
jossle	jostle	Jurrasic	Jurassic
joul	jowl	jurror	juror
joull	joule	jurry-rigged	jury-rigged
joviel	jovial	jusstafy	justify
jowst	joust	juvanile	juvenile
joye	joey (animal)	juxtepose	juxtapose
joyfull	joyful	jymnist	gymnast
joyuss	joyous	jynacollogy	gynecology
jubalee	jubilee	kabbob	kabob
jubalent	jubilant	kabbuky	Kabuki
jubbalation	jubilation	kacky	khaki
Juddaism	Judaism	kadish	kaddish

Incorrect	Correct	Incorrect	Correct
kael	kale	karrkool	karakul
kaffeeclatch	kaffeeklatsch	kartoon	cartoon
Kafkaesk	Kafkaesque	kashoe	cashew
kahki	khaki	katch	ketch (boat)
kairn	cairn	kaul	caul
kakimono	kakemono	Kaynsian	Keynesian
kakostochracy	kakistocracy	kayoss	chaos
kalazea	chalaza	kaysadilla	quesadilla
Kaldean	Chaldean	kayyak	kayak
kalidascope	kaleidoscope	kazm	chasm
kallus	callous (uncaring) or callus (thick skin)	kechup	ketchup
		kedje	kedge
		keelbasa	kielbasa
kamelleon	chameleon	keesh	quiche
Kammasutra	Kama Sutra	keestone	keystone
kanter	canter	keewee	kiwi
kaola	koala	kelo	kilo
kapock	kapok	kelpe	kelp
kapoot	kaput	Kelvan	Kelvin
karaff	carafe	kemmist	chemist
karies	caries	kennell	kennel
karisma	charisma	keosk	kiosk
karnashun	carnation	keppi	kepi
karnel	carnal	kercheif	kerchief
karomba	caramba	kernul	colonel (officer)
karot	carat (jewel weight)	kernul	kernel (core)
		kerratin	keratin
karot	karat (gold measure)	Kerron	Charon
		kestral	kestrel
karrat	carat (jewel weight)	Ketchuan	Quechuan
		kettel	kettle
karrat	karat (gold measure)	ketzell	quetzal
		Keyeve	Kiev
		Khmeer	Khmer

Incorrect	Correct	Incorrect	Correct
khnish	knish	klone	clone
kiasmsus	chiasmus	klorene	chlorine
kibbits	kibitz (meddle)	kloride	chloride
kibutz	kibbutz (settlement)	kloroform	chloroform
		Klu Klux Klan	Ku Klux Klan
Kidush	Kiddush	klutch	clutch
kikshaw	kickshaw	knapsac	knapsack
killhaul	keelhaul	kneid	knead
Killimanjaro	Kilimanjaro	knickname	nickname
kimona	kimono	knicnack	knickknack
kindergarden	kindergarten	knockneed	knock-kneed
kindrid	kindred	knowlege	knowledge
kinkijou	kinkajou	koax	coax
kinnetic	kinetic	koche	coach
kirn	kern	Kodeak	Kodiak
kiromansy	chiromancy	koen	koan
kiropractik	chiropractic	koeshur	kosher
kirrography	chirography	koff	cough
kiser	kaiser	koffer	coffer
kismett	kismet	kofferdam	cofferdam
ki-square	chi-square	koko	cocoa
kitsh	kitsch	koleslaw	coleslaw
kittchen	kitchen	kolesterol	cholesterol
klannish	clannish	kolleric	choleric
klarion	clarion	kolrabi	kohlrabi
klasp	clasp	konk	conk (a blow)
klaut	clout	konk	conch (a shell)
klavays	claves	kookoo	cuckoo
klaw hammar	claw hammer	koop	coop (pen)
kleeg	klieg	kooskus	couscous
kleet	cleat	koot	coot
kleff	clef	koo-ture	couture
kleptamaniac	kleptomaniac	korale	chorale
klezzmer	klezmer	kord	chord

Incorrect	Correct	Incorrect	Correct
koreopsis	coreopsis	kronnical	chronicle
korgy	corgi	kronograf	chronograph
korm	corm	kronollogy	chronology
korneesh	corniche	kronological	chronological
kornet	cornet	krotch	crotch
korniss	cornice	krout	kraut
korr	corps	krunch	crunch
korragraf	choreograph	kudose	kudos
korrea	chorea	kue	cue
korrus	chorus	kurchif	kerchief
kortaje	cortege	kusp	cusp
koupe	coupe (car)	kuspid	cuspid
kowl	cowl	kwala	koala
kracken	kraken	kwalm	qualm
krampun	crampon	kweasy	queasy
kranny	cranny	kwell	quell
Kremmlen	Kremlin	kwench	quench
krepuscular	crepuscular	kwest	quest
kresh	creche	kwetzel	quetzal
krick	crick	kwid	quid
kript	crypt	kwid pro kwo	quid pro quo
kripton	krypton	kwidnunk	quidnunc
krisanthamum	chrysanthemum	kwietuss	quietus
krisote	creosote	kwill	quill
krissalis	chrysalis	kwince	quince
krocuss	crocus	kwinella	quinella
kromatic	chromatic	kwip	quip
kromatin	chromatin	kwirk	quirk
kromatograffy	chromatography	kwirt	quirt
krome	chrome	kwonsit	quonset
kronic	chronic	kwote	quote

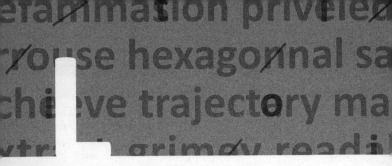

Most Commonly Misspelled Words

- laboratory
- laundry
- length
- library
- license
- lieu
- likelihood
- linoleum
- loneliness
- lying

Incorrect	Correct	Incorrect	Correct
labarynth	labyrinth	lampoone	lampoon
labborious	laborious	landaw	landau
laber	labor	langarus	languorous
Laberador	Labrador	langauge	language
laberatory	laboratory	langwid	languid
laberinth	labyrinth	langwish	languish
lable	label	lanjeray	lingerie
labrinth	labyrinth	lanlubber	landlubber
labrynthine	labyrinthine	lannia	lanai
lacconic	laconic	lanniard	lanyard
laccuna	lacuna	lannolin	lanolin
lach	latch	lanse	lance
lachramose	lachrymose	lantanna	lantana
lackadasical	lackadaisical	lanyap	lagniappe
lacker	lacquer	lappadary	lapidary
lacktate	lactate	lappis lazooli	lapis lazuli
lacktose	lactose	lappse	lapse
lacluster	lackluster	lappstrake	lapstrake
lacross	lacrosse	lapracaun	leprechaun
ladel	ladle	laquer	lacquer
laeth	lath (strip)	laringitis	laryngitis
laety	laity	larinks	larynx
laff	laugh	larjess	largess
laffable	laughable	larreate	laureate
laffter	laughter	larres and pennates	lares and penates
laggerd	laggard	larrva	larva (singular)
laggoon	lagoon	larseny	larceny
lam	lamb	larvee	larvae (plural)
lamda	lambda	larynks	larynx
lamma	lama (priest)	lasar	laser
lamma	llama (beast)	lascivvious	lascivious
lammanate	laminate	lasserate	lacerate
lammanation	lamination	lassez-fair	laissez-faire
lamment	lament	latecks	latex

Incorrect	Correct	Incorrect	Correct
latere	later (afterward)	leesure	leisure
latere	latter (last of two)	leetmotif	leitmotif
lathar	lather	legaslation	legislation
latine	lateen	leggality	legality
latint	latent	leggato	legato
latitudinarrean	latitudinarian	legibel	legible
latreen	latrine	legitimet	legitimate
lattise	lattice	legoom	legume
lattitude	latitude	leich	leach (drain)
laudible	laudable	leige	liege
laughtar	laughter	lein	lien
laun	lawn	lekchure	lecture
laundrymat	laundromat	lembo	limbo
laural	laurel	lemen	lemon
lavetory	lavatory	lemmeng	lemmlng
lavva	lava	lemmur	lemur
lawd	laud	lempid	limpid
lawdable	laudable	lench	lynch
lawnch	launch	lenght	length
layet	layette	lengua franka	lingua franca
laythe	lathe (machine)	lenoleum	linoleum
lazanga	lasagna	lentill	lentil
lazzaret	lazaret	lentisimo	lentissimo
leasure	leisure	lenyunt	lenient
lechary	lechery	leonnine	leonine
lecturn	lectern	lepard	leopard
ledd	led	leperous	leprous
lede	lead	leppard	leopard
ledgerdemane	legerdemain	lepresy	leprosy
leeche	leech (worm)	lerch	lurch
leegue	league	lesbean	lesbian
leeotard	leotard	lespedesa	lespedeza
leesay	lycee	lessez-faire	laissez-faire

Incorrect	Correct	Incorrect	Correct
letharjic	lethargic	liggature	ligature
lethel	lethal	ligiment	ligament
lether	leather	likelyhood	likelihood
lettis	lettuce	likker	liquor
leud	lewd	lilack	lilac
leveredge	leverage	lillee	lily
levitty	levity	lillipushun	lilliputian
levvatate	levitate	limbec	limbic
levven	leaven	limelite	limelight
levvy	levee	limenal	liminal
lexacon	lexicon	limm	limn
lianna	liana	limmitation	limitation
liarbird	lyrebird	limmrick	limerick
liason	liaison	limozine	limousine
libbertarean	libertarian	limph	lymph
libeedo	libido	linchpen	linchpin
liberel	liberal	lindin	linden
liberry	library	linement	lineament (outline)
liberteen	libertine		
lible	liable (responsible for)	linement	liniment (medicine)
lible	libel (defamation)	linin	linen
		linjerie	lingerie
libral	liberal	linkidge	linkage
librery	library	linneage	lineage
libreto	libretto	linnear	linear
licence	license	linnen	linen
licentishus	licentious	linnidge	lineage
licorish	licorice	linniment	lineament (outline)
lieble	liable		
liederkrans	liederkranz	linniment	liniment (medicine)
lier	liar		
lieutenent	lieutenant	linnoleum	linoleum

Incorrect	Correct	Incorrect	Correct
lintell	lintel	loiss	loess
lipp	lip	loitter	loiter
liqudate	liquidate	lome	loam
liquer	liqueur	londer	launder
liquify	liquefy	londromat	laundromat
liric	lyric	lonelyness	loneliness
liscense	license	longituddinal	longitudinal
lite	light	longuer	longueur
litening	lightning (bolt)	lonjevity	longevity
literatti	literati	loobricate	lubricate
literery	literary	looloo	lulu
litergy	liturgy	loone	loon
lithagraph	lithograph	lootheir	luthier
Lithuanea	Lithuania	loou	lieu
litmas	litmus	looze	lose
litotees	litotes	lornette	lorgnette
littany	litany	lorrey	lorry
litteral	literal (actual)	lothe	loath
litteral	littoral (shore)	lotis	lotus
litterature	literature	loundery	laundry
litthium	lithium	loupp	loupe
littigate	litigate	lownge	lounge
livelyhood	livelihood	lowquacious	loquacious
liverie	livery	lowthe	loathe (verb)
liverworst	liverwurst	lozinge	lozenge
livily	lively	lubracate	lubricate
lizzard	lizard	lubriccity	lubricity
loar	lore	lucretive	lucrative
lobatomy	lobotomy	ludacrous	ludicrous
locc	loch (lake)	Ludite	Luddite
locc	lock (to secure)	lued	lewd
loggarithm	logarithm	luekemia	leukemia
logisticks	logistics	lugage	luggage

Incorrect	Correct	Incorrect	Correct
lugubreous	lugubrious	lunchon	luncheon
lukemia	leukemia	luner	lunar
lulliby	lullaby	lupuce	lupus
lumenescent	luminescent	luschious	luscious
luminery	luminary	lutenant	lieutenant
luminus	luminous	luthear	luthier
lummenescence	luminescence	luxurience	luxuriance
lunasy	lunacy	lyracism	lyricism

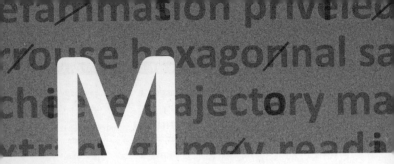

Most Commonly Misspelled Words

- macaroni
- magnitude
- maintenance
- marriage
- merciless
- mesmerize
- miniature
- mischievous
- misspell
- mysterious

Incorrect	Correct	Incorrect	Correct
macaber	macabre	maggistrate	magistrate
macaddam	macadam	maggit	maggot
macau	macaw (bird)	maggma	magma
MacBeath	Macbeth	maggnate	magnate
Maccabees	Macabees	maggneto	magneto
maccadamia	macadamia	magiccian	magician
maccarony	macaroni	maginta	magenta
maccaroon	macaroon	magnafication	magnification
maccrocosm	macrocosm	magnafy	magnify
Macedonnia	Macedonia	magnam	magnum
machinry	machinery	magnanimmity	magnanimity
machismoe	machismo	magnannamous	magnanimous
machoe	macho	magnatude	magnitude
Mackanaw	Mackinac (place) or Mackinaw (coat)	magnem opis	magnum opus
		magneseum	magnesium
		magnett	magnet
mackerral	mackerel	mahoggany	mahogany
mackination	machination	maile	mail (letters)
mackrocosm	macrocosm	maile	male (gender)
macramay	macramé	maime	maim
madamoiselle	mademoiselle	mainne	main (major)
maddonna	madonna	maintainance	maintenance
Madeera	Madeira	maintane	maintain
madragal	madrigal	maintanence	maintenance
madres	madras	maistro	maestro
mael	mail (letters)	majenta	magenta
mael	male (gender)	majer dommo	major domo
maelstrum	maelstrom	majestrate	magistrate
maen	main (major)	Maji	Magi
maen	mane (hair)	majollica	majolica
Maffea	Mafia	ma-jong	mah jongg (or jong)
Mafiosso	Mafioso		
Magdelene	Magdalene	majoret	majorette
magestereal	magisterial	majorrity	majority

Incorrect	Correct	Incorrect	Correct
makette	maquette	manganise	manganese
makewait	makeweight	Manks	Manx
makey	maquis	manlyness	manliness
makko	mako	mann	main (major)
makrocosm	macrocosm		mane (hair)
mal di mer	mal de mer		
maladrout	maladroit	mannacle	manacle
malakite	malachite	mannatee	manatee
malanzhe	mélange	manniac	maniac
malaze	malaise	mannic	manic
malestorm	maelstrom	mannicure	manicure
malevalent	malevolent	mannipulate	manipulate
malfactor	malefactor	manno a manno	mano a mano
malfeasince	malfeasance	mannor	manor (house)
malignency	malignancy	mannor	manner (method)
malignent	malignant	mannslaughter	manslaughter
malishia	militia	mannumit	manumit
malladiction	malediction	manoover	maneuver
malladroit	maladroit	mantenance	maintenance
mallaguena	malagueña	manuver	maneuver
mallamute	malamute	manyfold	manifold
mallapropism	malapropism	manyure	manure
mallaria	malaria	maraca	maraca
malledy	malady	marashino	maraschino
mallerd	mallard	maratime	maritime
mallevalance	malevolent	marcacite	marcasite
malliable	malleable	Mardi Gra	Mardi Gras
mallice	malice	margenal	marginal
Malthusean	Malthusian	marginelize	marginalize
mammba	mamba	margurita	margarita
mammbo	mambo	mariachee	mariachi
manackle	manacle	mariwanna	marijuana
mandable	mandible	marjarine	margarine
mandalin	mandolin	marjorram	marjoram
		markee	marquee

Incorrect	Correct	Incorrect	Correct
marlen	marlin	massakism	masochism
marmallade	marmalade	massakistic	masochistic
marmut	marmot	masscot	mascot
marrage	marriage	massoose	masseuse
marrathon	marathon	masstacate	masticated
marrauder	marauder	masstadon	mastodon
marrigold	marigold	masstif	mastiff
marrimba	marimba	massuer	masseur
marrina	marina	mastadon	mastodon
marrinade	marinade	mastectamy	mastectomy
marrinara	marinara	masterbate	masturbate
marrinate	marinate	masterbatiion	masturbation
marrischino	maraschino	mastick	mastic
marritime	maritime	mastitus	mastitis
marshel	marshal (guide)	mastro	maestro
marshel	Marshall (islands)	mathamatical	mathematical
marshel	martial (warlike)	matinay	matinee
marshell	martial	matramony	matrimony
marshmellow	marshmallow	matraside	matricide
marsipan	marzipan	matre di	maitre d'
marsoupial	marsupial	matrearch	matriarch
marter	martyr	matress	mattress
marvellous	marvelous	matricks	matrix
marygold	marigold	matricullate	matriculate
masachism	masochism	mattador	matador
mascarra	mascara	matter famillias	materfamilias
masculen	masculine	matterialism	materialism
mase	mace	matternal	maternal
masheen	machine	mattzo ball	matzo ball
mashetty	machete	maturration	maturation
mashination	machination	maudlen	maudlin
maskarade	masquerade	maukish	mawkish
massadje	massage	mausolium	mausoleum
massaker	massacre	mawl	maul

Incorrect	Correct	Incorrect	Correct
maxxim	maxim	meggahurts	megahertz
maxximize	maximize	meggalomania	megalomania
maya culpa	mea culpa	meitosis	mitosis
mayhim	mayhem	melatonine	melatonin
mayoh	maillot	mellancolly	melancholy
mayonase	mayonnaise	mellange	melange
mazzerd	mazzard	mellanoma	melanoma
mazzurka	mazurka	mellifluus	mellifluous
McAdam	macadam	mellioration	melioration
meagger	meager	mellodrama	melodrama
meandor	meander	mellodramatic	melodramatic
measureable	measurable	mellungean	Melungeon
measurment	measurement	membrain	membrane
mechinism	mechanism	meminto	memento
Mecka	Mecca	memmoir	memoir
medalleon	medallion	memmorandom	memorandum
meddean	median	memmorial	memorial
meddication	medication	mendaceous	mendacious
meddieval	medieval	mennace	menace
meddiocre	mediocre	mennage a troi	menage a trois
meddley	medley	mennagery	menagerie
meddlist	medalist	menndicant	mendicant
meddow	meadow	menniel	menial
mediun	median	menningitis	meningitis
meed	mead	menniscus	meniscus
meeger	meager	mennora	menorah
meercat	meerkat	menstrate	menstruate
meete	meat (flesh), meet (join), mete (give out)	menstration	menstruation
		mentel	mental
		menter	mentor
meeterology	meteorology	menustration	menstruation
meezles	measles	mercanteel	mercantile
meezly	measly	mercureal	mercurial
Meffastofales	Mephistopheles	mercyless	merciless

Incorrect	Correct	Incorrect	Correct
merengay	merengué (dance)	mettamorfasus	metamorphosis
		mettaphor	metaphor
Merkator	Mercator	mettastasize	metastasize
merlo	merlot	mettatarsel	metatarsal
mermade	mermaid	mettelsome	mettlesome
merrang	meringue (topping)	metteor	meteor
		metticulous	meticulous
merratocracy	meritocracy	mettric	metric
merratricious	meretricious	metzo-soprano	mezzo-soprano
merridian	meridian	mezzinine	mezzanine
merrygold	marigold	mia culpa	mea culpa
merschaum	meerschaum	miccron	micron
mescalline	mescaline	micrabiology	microbiology
mesmerise	mesmerize	micracosm	microcosm
messanger	messenger	microfish	microfiche
messcal	mescal	microfone	microphone
messianick	messianic	micturishion	micturition
messiuh	messiah	micturrate	micturate
messquite	mesquite	midgit	midget
messyness	messiness	midrif	midriff
metabbalism	metabolism	mielieu	milieu
metaphore	metaphor	mige	midge
metastacize	metastasize	migrain	migraine
metemorphisus	metamorphosis	migrattory	migratory
Methadust	Methodist	milage	mileage
methamfettamine		millanary	millinery
	methamphetamine	millenium	millennium
methidone	methadone	millenneum	millennium
methodicle	methodical	millionair	millionaire
metranome	metronome	millitant	militant
metrapolitan	metropolitan	millitate	militate
metropollis	metropolis	millitery	military
mettabolic	metabolic	milue	milieu
mettalick	metallic	mimeesus	mimesis

Incorrect	Correct	Incorrect	Correct
mimmic	mimic	missionery	missionary
mimmosa	mimosa	Missisippi	Mississippi
miniscule	minuscule	misslead	mislead or misled (past tense)
ministroane	minestrone		
minnataur	minotaur		
minnature	miniature	missleading	misleading
minneral	mineral	missletoe	mistletoe
minnimel	minimal	missnomer	misnomer
minnion	minion	misspronunciacion	mispronunciation
minniscule	minuscule	misterious	mysterious
minnister	minister	mistical	mystical
minnority	minority	mistique	mystique
minstral	minstrel	mitar	miter
minuette	minuet	mithical	mythical
miopic	myopic	mithollogy	mythology
miossis	meiosis	mittagate	mitigate
miread	myriad	mitzva	mitzvah
mirmaid	mermaid	mizer	miser
mirraculous	miraculous	moantage	montage
Mirranda	Miranda	moate	moat (ditch)
mirrh	myrrh	moate	mote (dust speck)
mischavus	mischievous		
misdemener	misdemeanor	mobalize	mobilize
Mishagan	Michigan	mobillity	mobility
mishapen	misshapen	Mobius stripp	Moebius strip
mishun	mission	moccasin	moccasin
misille	missile	mock number	mach number
misogeny	misogyny	modallaty	modality
mispell	misspell	moddal	modal
mispronounse	mispronounce	modderate	moderate
missalany	miscellany	moddernaty	modernity
missel	missile	moddernism	modernism
misselanious	miscellaneous	moddest	modest
missenthrope	misanthrope	moddify	modify

Incorrect	Correct	Incorrect	Correct
moddular	modular	monomannia	monomania
modecum	modicum	mononucleossis	mononucleosis
modren	modern	monopallize	monopolize
modullate	modulate	monotheistick	monotheistic
moduss operanda	modus operandi	monseur	monsieur
moehair	mohair	monstrossity	monstrosity
moeped	moped	monstruss	monstrous
moitty	moiety	monsune	monsoon
mokka	mocha	Montassori	Montessori
molecullar	molecular	montazhe	montage
mollafy	mollify	moo gooh guy pan	moo goo gai pan
mollases	molasses	moosse	moose (animal)
Mollatov cocktail	Molotov cocktail	moosse	mousse (dessert)
		mooton	mouton
moller	molar	mootual	mutual
mollest	molest	morbiddity	morbidity
mollybdenim	molybdenum	morf	morph
momenterry	momentary	morfeen	morphine
monaglot	monoglot	morfeme	morpheme
monarky	monarchy	morfollagy	morphology
mondigrean	mondegreen	morgage	mortgage
moneterry	monetary	morral	moral (ethical)
mongral	mongrel	morral	morale (attitude)
monnacle	monocle	morrel	morel (mushroom)
monnaker	monicker		
monnalog	monologue	morras	morass
monnarch	monarch	Morravian	Moravian
monnasyllabel	monosyllable	morray ele	moray eel
monnater	monitor	morrel	moral (ethical)
monniker	moniker	morrel	morale (attitude)
monnitor	monitor	morrel	morel (mushroom)
monnotonous	monotonous		
monocromatic	monochromatic	morrell	moral (ethical)
monogammy	monogamy	morrell	morale (attitude)

Incorrect	Correct	Incorrect	Correct
morrell	morel (mushroom)	muckus	mucous (adj)
		muckus	mucus (noun)
morron	moron	mucobb	macabre
morsell	morsel	muffel	muffle
mortafy	mortify	muffty	mufti
mortallity	mortality	muggwump	mugwump
mortel	mortal	mukraker	muckraker
morter	mortar	mullato	mulatto
mortishian	mortician	mullit	mullet
mortiss	mortise	mulluh	mullah
mortuarry	mortuary	multameddia	multimedia
mosaik	mosaic	multaprocesser	multiprocessor
moshun	motion	multiplacation	multiplication
mosk	mosque	mummor	mummer
mosquetto	mosquito	mundain	mundane
mosquetos	mosquitoes	municiple	municipal
mossoleum	mausoleum	munissipality	municipality
moteef	motif	munnificent	munificent
Mother Terresa	Mother Teresa	Munnster	Muenster
mottley	motley	muree	murre
Motzart	Mozart	murge	merge
moudem	modem	murlow	merlot
mountybank	mountebank	murmer	murmur
mournfull	mournful	murrh	myrrh
mouss	moose (animal)	murth	mirth
mouss	mousse (dessert)	musculer	muscular
mout	moot	muscullature	musculature
mouthfull	mouthful	museam	museum
movvable	movable	museli	muesli
mozaic	mosaic	musillage	mucilage
Mozlim	Muslim	muskalunge	muskellunge
mucillage	mucilage	muskateer	musketeer
muckous	mucous (adj)	muskit	musket
muckous	mucus (noun)	muskmellon	muskmelon

Incorrect	Correct	Incorrect	Correct
Muslem	Muslim	myoot	mute
musscadine	muscadine	myootation	mutation
musscatel	muscatel	myoppathy	myopathy
musscle	muscle	myoppic	myopic
musster	muster	myosis	meiosis
mustash	mustache	myreid	myriad
musterd	mustard	myrr	myrrh
mutent	mutant	mysteek	mystique
muttilate	mutilate	mystereous	mysterious
muttiny	mutiny	mysticle	mystical
muzeam	museum	mythacal	mythical
muzzel	muzzle	mythollogy	mythology
myaloma	myeloma	myutate	mutate

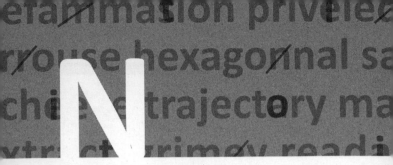

Most Commonly Misspelled Words

- naïve
- narcissistic
- nauseous
- necessary
- neighborly
- neither
- niece
- noticeable
- nourish
- nutrition

Incorrect	Correct	Incorrect	Correct
nabbulus	nebulous	nauttical	nautical
naccer	nacre	nautty	naughty
nader	nadir	nauw	gnaw
naeve	naïve	navvagator	navigator
naevetay	naivete	Navvaho	Navajo
nannosecond	nanosecond	navval	naval (sea), navel (belly)
napken	napkin		
nappalm	napalm	navvel	naval (sea), navel (belly)
napsack	knapsack		
napthalene	naphthalene	navvigable	navigable
naration	narration	navvigation	navigation
narcallepsy	narcolepsy	nawing	gnawing
narcissis	narcissus	nayad	naiad
narkosis	narcosis	nayberly	neighborly
narkotic	narcotic	naybob	nabob
narl	gnarl	naybor	neighbor
nascents	nascence	nayborhood	neighborhood
nascistic	narcissistic	nealogism	neologism
nasel	nasal	Neandorthal	Neanderthal
nasent	nascent	Neapollitan	Neapolitan
nashe	gnash	neauveau	nouveau
Nassaw	Nassau	nebbula	nebula
nasturshum	nasturtium	neccraphilia	necrophilia
natcho	nacho	necesary	necessary
natent	natant	necessatate	necessitate
nativvatty	nativity	neckerchef	neckerchief
natt	gnat	neckramancy	necromancy
nattal	natal	necktur	nectar
naturallize	naturalize	necrollagy	necrology
naturallizm	naturalism	necrossis	necrosis
nausiated	nauseated	neep tide	neap tide
nausious	nauseous	neet's foot oil	neat's-foot oil
naut	naught	neffarious	nefarious
nautillus	nautilus	Neffertiti	Nefertiti

Incorrect	Correct	Incorrect	Correct
neggate	negate	neutreno	neutrino
negglazhay	negligee	neverthaless	nevertheless
neglagent	negligent	newbile	nubile
negociable	negotiable	newell post	newel post
neice	niece	newmattic	pneumatic
neighberly	neighborly	newmonia	pneumonia
nell	knell	newron	neuron
nembus	nimbus	newrosis	neurosis
nemmasis	nemesis	newrotransmitter	neurotransmitter
nemmatoad	nematode	newrottic	neurotic
nenja	ninja	newrottically	neurotically
neoconservitive	neoconservative	newsance	nuisance
neolitthick	neolithic	newter	neuter
neonatollogy	neonatology	newtral	neutral
neoplastee	neoplasty	newtrition	nutrition
nephrittis	nephritis	newtritionist	nutritionist
nepinthee	nepenthe	newtron	neutron
ne pluss ultrah	ne plus ultra	nexxus	nexus
neppatism	nepotism	ney	née (born)
Neptoon	Neptune	ney	neigh (sound made by a horse)
nervus	nervous		
neshient	nescient		
nessel	nestle	niccoteen	nicotine
Nesstor	Nestor	Niceen	Nicene
nethar	nether	niceniss	niceness
nettel	nettle	nickle	nickel
Neufshattel	Neufchatel	nickleodion	nickelodeon
neuralgea	neuralgia	nicktate	nictate
neurel	neural	niegh	neigh (sound made by a horse)
neuresthennia	neuresthenia		
neurollagy	neurology	niesce	gneiss
neurropathy	neuropathy	niether	neither
neurrotransmittor	neurotransmitter	niggardally	niggardly
neutrallaty	neutrality	nighte	night

Incorrect	Correct	Incorrect	Correct
nihalism	nihilism	nondenomminational	
nimbel	nimble		nondenominational
nimbuss	nimbus	nonendity	nonentity
nimmrod	nimrod	nonenvassive	noninvasive
nimph	nymph	nonpareel	nonpareil
nippel	nipple	nonpartison	nonpartisan
nirvanna	nirvana	nonprolifferation	nonproliferation
nish	niche	nonshallant	nonchalant
nitche	niche	Norweegian	Norwegian
nitragin	nitrogen	nosstalgia	nostalgia
nitroglyceran	nitroglycerin	nosstrum	nostrum
noame	gnome	nostic	Gnostic
Nobell	Nobel	Nostradommus	Nostradamus
nobell	noble	notafy	notify
nobillity	nobility	noticable	noticeable
nocchi	gnocchi	notoreous	notorious
nockworst	knackwurst	notoriaty	notoriety
nocturn	nocturne	nouggat	nougat
nocturnel	nocturnal	nouvou reche	nouveau riche
nollo condender	nolo contendere	novisheate	novitiate
nomen	gnomon	novvel	novel
nommad	nomad	novvelty	novelty
nomme de guer	nom de guerre	noxxous	noxious
nomme de plume	nom de plume	nuclius	nucleus
nommenclature	nomenclature	nucular	nuclear
nomminal	nominal	nuddaty	nudity
nommination	nomination	nuddge	nudge
nomminative	nominative	nue	gnu
nonchelonse	nonchalance	nugatorry	nugatory
noncombattent	noncombatant	nulification	nullification
non compass mentus	non compos mentis	nullafy	nullify
		numismattist	numismatist
non seqquitor	non sequitur	numm	numb
noncupative	nuncupative	nummerator	numerator

Incorrect	Correct	Incorrect	Correct
nummerel	numeral	nursary	nursery
nummin	numen	nurturre	nurture
numminous	numinous	nusance	nuisance
numonic	mnemonic	nutrea	nutria
nupshial	nuptial	nutreant	nutrient
nurrish	nourish	nutrittion	nutrition
nurrishment	nourishment	nymfomania	nymphomania

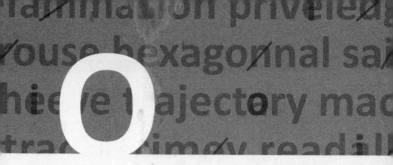

Most Commonly Misspelled Words

- obedient
- occasion
- odyssey
- official
- omission
- opposite
- optimism
- orangutan
- ordinary
- ought

Incorrect	Correct	Incorrect	Correct
oassis	oasis	obveate	obviate
obay	obey	occassion	occasion
obbalisk	obelisk	occassionaly	occasionally
obblate	oblate	Occedent	Occident
obbligate	obligate	occidentel	occidental
obbligatorry	obligatory	occippital	occipital
obbliterate	obliterate	occludding	occluding
obblong	oblong	occlussion	occlusion
obderate	obdurate	occuler	ocular
obediant	obedient	occulist	oculist
obeese	obese	occupasion	occupation
obituery	obituary	occupunt	occupant
objeccion	objection	occurence	occurrence
objectivvaty	objectivity	ocker	ochre
objett da arte	objet d'art	ockerina	ocarina
obligging	obliging	ockult	occult
oblike	oblique	oclock	o'clock
oblivviate	obliviate	octagenarian	octogenarian
obnoxxious	obnoxious	octaggon	octagon
obsalete	obsolete	octapus	octopus
obseen	obscene	oddyssy	odyssey
obsequeus	obsequious	odeum	odium
observasion	observation	odiferous	odoriferous
observent	observant	odius	odious
obsesion	obsession	odommater	odometer
obsesive	obsessive	Oedapus	Oedipus
obsiddean	obsidian	oeth	oath
obsolessent	obsolescent	offel	offal
obssennaty	obscenity	offen	often
obstannite	obstinate	offeratory	offertory
obstetricks	obstetrics	offishal	official
obstickle	obstacle	ofthalmollogy	ophthalmology
obstrepperous	obstreperous	oger	ogre
obtoose	obtuse	oggel	ogle

Incorrect	Correct	Incorrect	Correct
oh pair	au pair	oover	oeuvre
oh revoire	au revoir	oozo	ouzo
oister	oyster	opake	opaque
olfactery	olfactory	opassity	opacity
oliomargarine	oleomargarine	operrata	operetta
olligarchy	oligarchy	operratic	operatic
ollio	olio	ophthalmollogy	ophthalmology
omboushure	embouchure	oppera	opera
ombuddsman	ombudsman	oppertunety	opportunity
omenious	ominous	oppertunist	opportunist
omfally	omphali	oppine	opine
Omish	Amish	oppinionated	opinionated
ommelet	omelet	oppisite	opposite
ommission	omission	oppium	opium
ommitt	omit	opponant	opponent
omnippatent	omnipotent	opposed	opposed
omnishent	omniscient	oppossum	opossum
omnivverous	omnivorous	opprobreum	opprobrium
omnydirectional	omnidirectional	opptical	optical
onamottomania	onomatomania	oppulence	opulence
onclave	enclave	oppulent	opulent
oncollagist	oncologist	oppune	oppugn
oncte	once	opression	oppression
onnus	onus	optamism	optimism
onomattopeia	onomatopoeia	optamistic	optimistic
onsemble	ensemble	optamum	optimum
onsomble	ensemble	opuscalum	opusculum
onterage	entourage	orangutang	orangutan
ontollogical	ontological	orbittal	orbital
ontree	entrée	orcastrate	orchestrate
onvoy	envoy	orchestera	orchestra
oomeak	umiak or oomiak	orckid	orchid
oomff	oomph	ordanance	ordnance (weaponry)
oomlout	umlaut		

Incorrect	Correct	Incorrect	Correct
ordanance	ordinance (local law)	osstrich	ostrich
		ostensably	ostensibly
ordane	ordain	ostentacious	ostentatious
ordenance	ordinance	osteoporrosis	osteoporosis
ordinnary	ordinary	ostinsable	ostensible
oreggano	oregano	ostiopath	osteopath
organnic	organic	ostrocize	ostracize
orgasem	orgasm	ounse	ounce
orgassmic	orgasmic	outgoeing	outgoing
orgey	orgy	outragious	outrageous
origommy	origami	outray	outré
orijin	origin	outway	outweigh
ornamintal	ornamental	ovarien	ovarian
ornathology	ornithology	overry	ovary
orrientation	orientation	overtoor	overture
orrigamy	origami	overun	overrun
orringe	orange	overwhilming	overwhelming
orrison	orison	ovull	oval
orrotund	orotund	ovva	ova
orthadox	orthodox	ovvation	ovation
orthodonticks	orthodontics	ovvert	overt
orthoggraphy	orthography	ovvulate	ovulate
orthopeddics	orthopedics	ovvulation	ovulation
oskulate	osculate	ovvum	ovum
osmossis	osmosis	oxagen	oxygen
ossafication	ossification	oxxen	oxen
ossafy	ossify	oxxidation	oxidation
ossilate	oscillate	oxxone	oxone
ossillascope	oscilloscope	oystir	oyster
ossmosis	osmosis	ozmosis	osmosis

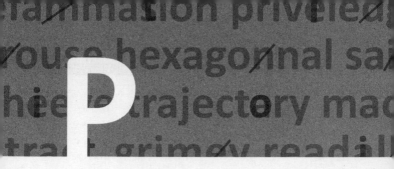

Most Commonly Misspelled Words

- parallel
- peculiar
- perceive
- permanent
- perseverance
- piece
- pleasant
- possess
- prejudice
- probably

Incorrect	Correct	Incorrect	Correct
pacience	patience	panarama	panorama
pack man	Pac man	panasea	panacea
packa	paca	pancreus	pancreas
packette	packet	pandamonium	pandemonium
packyderm	pachyderm	panetone	panettone
packysandra	pachysandra	pannatella	panetella
padedeux	pas de deux	panninni	panini
pagen	pagan	pannoply	panoply
pagiant	pageant	panser	panzer
pagiantry	pageantry	pantamime	pantomime
paine	pain (hurt)	panteloon	pantaloon
paine	pane (glass)	pantheeist	pantheist
pakastan	Pakistan	pantheeon	pantheon
palacial	palatial	panthor	panther
palatzo	palazzo	pantoom	pantoum
palempsest	palimpsest	panz nez	pince nez
palendrome	palindrome	papasy	papacy
palett	palate (taste)	papiruss	papyrus
palett	palette (artist's paintholder)	papparazzi	paparazzi
		parabollic	parabolic
palimino	palomino	paracide	parricide
paliontology	paleontology	paradice	paradise
palitable	palatable	paradime	paradigm
palital	palatal	parafin	paraffin
pallameno	palomino	paralax	parallax
pallate	palate	paralel	parallel
pallatial	palatial	paralize	paralyze
pallaver	palaver	parallysis	paralysis
palpatate	palpitate	paramoor	paramour
palpuble	palpable	paramutual	parimutuel
pampass	pampas	paranoya	paranoia
pamplet	pamphlet	parapalegic	paraplegic
panajyric	panegyric	paraphanalia	paraphernalia
panaply	panoply	parashute	parachute

Incorrect	Correct	Incorrect	Correct
parasight	parasite	passify	pacify
parasole	parasol	passionetely	passionately
paredy	parody	passtime	pastime
parenthisis	parenthesis	Pasternack	Pasternak
parfay	parfait	pastishe	pastiche
parhellion	parhelion	pasturize	pasteurize
parkay	parquet	patay	pate
parketry	parquetry	patchooli	patchouli
parkka	parka	pathegennic	pathogenic
parlence	parlance	pathollogy	pathology
parliment	parliament	pathose	pathos
Parmazan	Parmesan	patiserie	patisserie
Parnasus	Parnassus	patriarck	patriarch
paroxism	paroxysm	patronimic	patronymic
parquay	parquet	pattela	patella
parrabala	parabola	pattina	patina
parrable	parable	pattracide	patricide
parrameter	parameter	pattrician	patrician
parraplegic	paraplegic	patwa	patois
parrishoner	parishioner	pavillion	pavilion
parrott	parrot	pawper	pauper
parrsec	parsec	payella	paella
parshall	partial	paysano	paisano
parshally	partially	paytriot	patriot
parsnup	parsnip	peak	pique
parteeta	partita	peake	peak
partener	partner	pecadillo	peccadillo
Parthenen	Parthenon	pecteral	pectoral
partical	particle	peculear	peculiar
particuler	particular	pedacure	pedicure
parvenue	parvenu	pedagree	pedigree
pasifism	pacifism	pedament	pediment
passacaglea	passacaglia	pedastel	pedestal
passian	passion	ped-a-terre	pied-a-terre

Incorrect	Correct	Incorrect	Correct
peddagogue	pedagogue	pennuche	penuche
pederest	pederast	penoire	peignoir
peedmont	piedmont	penot	pinot
peek	pique	penshant	penchant
Peekanese	Pekingese	pentacostal	pentecostal
peeke	peek	pentatuke	pentateuch
peerege	peerage	pentical	pentacle
peerogue	pirogue	penus	penis
peerot	pierrot	peplam	peplum
peet	peat	pepperony	pepperoni
peetry dish	petri dish	per say	per se
Pegasous	Pegasus	peragative	prerogative
peice	piece	perambullate	perambulate
peity	piety	peranna	piranha
pejoritive	pejorative	perapetetic	peripatetic
peko	pekoe	peraphrasis	periphrasis
pel mell	pell mell	perastalsis	peristalsis
pellegra	pellagra	perastroika	perestroika
pellican	pelican	peratonitis	peritonitis
pemican	pemmican	percalle	percale
penacle	pinnacle	percapita	per capita
pendalum	pendulum	percentle	percentile
pendunt	pendant	perchase	purchase
penence	penance (atonement)	perchatelli	perciatelli
		percieve	perceive
penence	pinnace (boat)	perculate	percolate
penensula	peninsula	peremeter	perimeter
penent	pennant	peremptery	peremptory
pengwin	penguin	perequisite	prerequisite
penil	penal	perfunctery	perfunctory
penitance	penitence	perifary	periphery
pennetrate	penetrate	perimmeter	perimeter
pennetration	penetration	periodentics	periodontics
pennicilen	penicillin	perke	perk

Incorrect	Correct	Incorrect	Correct
perkolate	percolate	petrafy	petrify
perkwisit	perquisite	petrole	petrel (bird)
permanant	permanent	petrole	petrol (gas)
permiable	permeable	pettal	petal
permissable	permissible	pettraglyph	petroglyph
pernishus	pernicious	pewtrid	putrid
perqusit	perquisite	phayton	Phaethon (Greek god), phaeton (carriage)
perragrin	peregrine		
perrapatetic	peripatetic		
perrascope	periscope		
perrenial	perennial	phallas	phallus
perripheral	peripheral	phallick	phallic
perruse	peruse	Pharasee	Pharisee
perscription	prescription	pharmasootical	pharmaceutical
Persean	Persian	pharmasy	pharmacy
persentage	percentage	pharoh	pharaoh
perseverence	perseverance	phaze	faze (to disturb)
persimman	persimmon	phaze	phase (stage)
persistant	persistent	pheasent	pheasant
persistense	persistence	phebe	phoebe
persnicketty	persnickety	Phebus	Phoebus
personell	personnel	phenix	phoenix
perspecktive	perspective	phenominal	phenomenal
persperation	perspiration	phenommanon	phenomenon
perspickuity	perspicuity	phenugreek	fenugreek
persue	pursue	philataly	philately
perverrse	perverse	philenthropic	philanthropic
pessamism	pessimism	philestine	philistine
pessant	peasant	philhelenic	philhellenic
pessel	pestle	phillander	philander
pessery	pessary	phillipi	Philippi
pestilent	pestilent	Phillipines	Philippines
pestir	pester	phillistine	philistine
peton	piton	philodendren	philodendron

Incorrect	Correct	Incorrect	Correct
philum	phylum	pietta	pieta
phisical	physical	piggeon	pidgin (language)
phlebatemy	phlebotomy	piggeon	pigeon (bird)
phlegathon	Phlegethon	pilgram	pilgrim
phleghm	phlegm	pillaster	pilaster
phlegmattic	phlegmatic	Pillatees	Pilates
phonnetic	phonetic	piller	pillar
phonnic	phonic	pillfer	pilfer
phospherus	phosphorus	pillidge	pillage
phosphoresence	phosphorescence	pillot	pilot (one in charge)
photogennic	photogenic		
photosynthesis	photosynthesis	Pillot	Pilate (Roman prefect)
phrasology	phraseology		
phrenalogy	phrenology	pimpernal	pimpernel
phtisic	phthisic	pinchers	pincers
phylactery	phylactery	pinnion	pinion
phyrigean	Phrygian	pinser	pincer
physiccal	physical	piqque	pique
phyzisian	physician	pirasy	piracy
piannist	pianist	pirrogi	pierogi
piaza	piazza	pistacchio	pistachio
pibald	piebald	pithee	pithy
picata	piccata	pitifull	pitiful
piccalo	piccolo	pittence	pittance
piccaro	picaro	pittuitery	pituitary
pickalily	piccalilli	pixxel	pixel
Pickaneese	Pekingese	pizicatto	pizzicato
pickant	piquant	plaise	plaice (fish), place (location)
pickay	piqué (fabric)		
pickyune	picayune	placeebo	placebo
picnicing	picnicking	plackerd	placard
pictagraph	pictograph	plagerize	plagiarize
pidgeon	pidgin (language)	plaine	plain (simple)
pidgeon	pigeon (bird)	plaine	plane (flat)

Incorrect	Correct	Incorrect	Correct
planaterium	planetarium	poinsetta	poinsettia
planckton	plankton	poinyunsy	poignancy
planetiff	plaintiff	poisen	poison
plantin	plantain	polinaise	polonaise
plantir	plantar (sole of foot)	politbureau	politburo
		pollarize	polarize
plantive	plaintive	pollemic	polemic
plasenta	placenta	polligamy	polygamy
plasid	placid	polligon	polygon
plasteron	plastron	pollin	pollen
platapus	platypus	pollip	polyp
plattatude	platitude	pollitician	politician
plattinum	platinum	pollusion	pollution
playgue	plague	pollymath	polymath
playright	playwright	polyanna	pollyanna
pleadies	Pleiades	polywog	polliwog
pleasent	pleasant	pomagranite	pomegranate
pleazure	pleasure	pompador	pompadour
plebian	plebeian	Pompay	Pompeii
plee	plea	pompossity	pomposity
pleese	please	pompus	pompous
pleet	pleat	ponce-nay	pince-nez
plennary	plenary	ponsiana	poinciana
plentaful	plentiful	pontune	pontoon
plentatude	plenitude	poppenjay	popinjay
plummer	plumber	populus	populace
plummit	plummet	popuree	potpourri
plurisy	pleurisy	porchulakka	portulaca
plurral	plural	porkapine	porcupine
pneumattic	pneumatic	pornoggraphy	pornography
pneumonnia	pneumonia	porpise	porpoise
podietrist	podiatrist	porrige	porridge
pogram	pogrom	porselane	porcelain
poignent	poignant	porsion	portion

Incorrect	Correct	Incorrect	Correct
portind	portend	pretensious	pretentious
portint	portent	prevelent	prevalent
portkulas	portcullis	preye	prey (victim)
portrate	portrait	primative	primitive
portrey	portray	primerrily	primarily
posess	possess	primery	primary
possability	possibility	princeple	principal (main, person)
possesion	possession		
possey	posse	princeple	principle (rule)
posterier	posterior	principel	principal (main, person)
posthumus	posthumous		
potata	potato	principel	principle (rule)
potentialy	potentially	pristeen	pristine
pottary	pottery	privatision	privatization
prarie	prairie	priveledge	privilege
preciselly	precisely	privit	privet
predetory	predatory	privoke	provoke
predictible	predictable	privvatise	privatize
pre-deu	prie-dieu	prizm	prism
predjudice	prejudice	probaly	probably
preffered	preferred	probasion	probation
pre-fix	prix fixe	probossiss	proboscis
prejudise	prejudice	procede	proceed
premanition	premonition	proceedure	procedure
premeer	premiere	proclimation	proclamation
premice	premise	proclivitty	proclivity
preperation	preparation	Procrustees	Procrustes
presbaterian	Presbyterian	procter	proctor
preseed	precede	proctoscapy	proctoscopy
preshence	prescience	proctracter	protractor
preshent	prescient	proddagy	prodigy
presidence	precedence	prodiggious	prodigious
presperation	perspiration	profesion	profession
pressadent	precedent	professer	professor

Incorrect	Correct	Incorrect	Correct
profisient	proficient	pterodactal	pterodactyl
prohabition	prohibition	pubesent	pubescent
prohibitted	prohibited	publick	public
prologg	prologue	publickly	publicly
promanent	prominent	publisist	publicist
promennade	promenade	puerill	puerile
pronounsiation	pronunciation	puffan	puffin
propellant	propellent	pugnasious	pugnacious
prophassy	prophecy	pulchritood	pulchritude
propiciate	propitiate	pulkratudinous	pulchritudinous
proporsion	proportion	pullvarize	pulverize
propossal	proposal	pumise	pumice
proppaganda	propaganda	punative	punitive
proppeled	propelled	puppetery	puppetry
proprietery	proprietary	purchess	purchase
prosacution	prosecution	purda	purdah
proscutto	prosciutto	purmeate	permeate
prosennium	proscenium	purpel	purple
prossalite	proselyte	pursiflaje	persiflage
prosthettic	prosthetic	pursistant	persistent
protacol	protocol	purspicassity	perspicacity
proteens	proteins	purspicatious	perspicacious
provance	province	pursuent	pursuant
provenence	provenance	pusilannimous	pusillanimous
prudense	prudence	pussiance	puissance
pruderry	prudery	putative	putative
psaltary	psaltery	puter	pewter
pseudanym	pseudonym	putrafy	putrefy
pseudatorium	sudatorium	pwantalism	pointillism
psichiatrist	psychiatrist	pyorea	pyorrhea
psychedellic	psychedelic	pysisian	physician
psychosas	psychosis	pyschosis	psychosis
ptarmigun	ptarmigan	pysique	physique

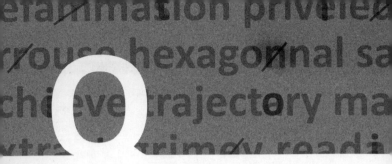

Most Commonly Misspelled Words

- quahog
- quantity
- quarrel
- quarter
- query
- quiet
- quite

Incorrect	Correct	Incorrect	Correct
Qoran	Koran, Qur'an	quartiel	quartile
quadraceps	quadriceps	quatrafoil	quatrefoil
quadralatteral	quadrilateral	quatrane	quatrain
quadraped	quadruped	quavver	quaver
quadrapleegic	quadriplegic	quazar	quasar
quadrattic	quadratic	que veev	qui vive
quadreel	quadrille	queassy	queasy
quadrent	quadrant	Quebeck	Quebec
quadrifonic	quadraphonic	quenssy	quinsy
quadrigessimel	quadragesimal	quentissential	quintessential
quadrilleon	quadrillion	quentupletts	quintuplets
quadroople	quadruple	querralous	querulous
quadrooplet	quadruplet	querry	quarry (mine)
quadrune	quadroon	querry	query (question)
quagmier	quagmire	quert	quart
quahogg	quahog	querty	QWERTY (keyboard)
quak	quack		
qualafication	qualification	quesh	quiche
qualaty	quality	questionaire	questionnaire
quale	quail	questionnible	questionable
quallify	qualify	quey	quay
quam	qualm	qui bono	cui bono
quandry	quandary	quiat	quiet (silent)
quantaffy	quantify	quiat	quite (very)
quantatative	quantitative	quibbel	quibble
quantaty	quantity	quid pro kwo	quid pro quo
quantem	quantum	quidnunk	quidnunc
Quantro	Cointreau	quier	quire
quarinteen	quarantine	quiessent	quiescent
quarrell	quarrel	quietas	quietus
quarrentine	quarantine	quinch	quench
quartar	quarter	quinnela	quinella
quartarmastar	quartermaster	quinnine	quinine
quartarnary	quaternary	quinquagennerean	quinquagenarian

Incorrect	Correct	Incorrect	Correct
quinqwinneal	quinquennial	quork	quark
quinse	quince	quortz	quartz
quintessance	quintessence	quosh	quash
quintilleon	quintillion	quosient	quotient
quintupple	quintuple	quotacion	quotation
quintupplet	quintuplet	quotible	quotable
quipp	quip	quotiddean	quotidian
quissling	quisling	quotta	quota
quitclame	quitclaim	qwad	quad
quivver	quiver	qwaint	quaint
quixxotic	quixotic	qwart	quart
quizes	quizzes	qwartet	quartet
quizine	cuisine	qwasadilla	quesadilla
quizzacle	quizzical	qwazi	quasi
quoen	quoin	qwetzel	quetzal
quoets	quoits	qwid	quid
quoff	quaff	qwirk	quirk
quoir	choir	qwirt	quirt
quondum	quondam	qwoff	quaff
quonsset	quonset	qwoth	quoth
quorem	quorum		

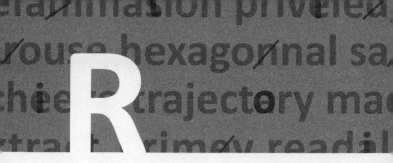

Most Commonly Misspelled Words

- raccoon
- radish
- raspberry
- raucous
- receive
- recommend
- religious
- repetition
- restaurant
- rhythm

Incorrect	Correct	Incorrect	Correct
Rabalaysian	Rabelaisian	**raggady**	raggedy
rabbel	rabble	**raggamuffin**	ragamuffin
rabbel-rouser	rabble-rouser	**raglen**	raglan
rabbid	rabid	**ragoo**	ragout
rabbinnical	rabbinical	**ragwart**	ragwort
rabbitt	rabbet (joint)	**railerry**	raillery
rabbitt	rabbit (animal)	**raill**	rale (breath sound)
rabeeze	rabies		
racey	racy	**raill**	rail (horizontal bar)
rachet	ratchet		
raciel	racial	**raille**	rale (breath sound), rail (horizontal bar)
racime	raceme		
racketear	racketeer		
rackitball	racquetball		
rackonture	raconteur	**raindeer**	reindeer
racoon	raccoon	**rainment**	raiment
radan	radon	**raisen**	raisin
raddar	radar	**raize**	raze
raddical	radical	**rakey**	reiki
raddient	radiant	**rakkish**	rakish
raddish	radish	**rallintando**	rallentando
radeal	radial	**raman**	ramen
radeate	radiate	**rambel**	ramble
radeum	radium	**Rambow**	Rimbaud (poet) Rambo (action hero)
radeus	radius		
radialogy	radiology		
radiater	radiator	**rambunkcious**	rambunctious
radiatter	radiator	**ramikin**	ramekin
radiel	radial	**Rammadan**	Ramadan
radience	radiance	**rammification**	ramification
radieye	radii	**rammpart**	rampart
radioissatope	radioisotope	**ramoulade**	remoulade
radiollogy	radiology	**rampaige**	rampage
raffel	raffle	**rampent**	rampant

Incorrect	Correct	Incorrect	Correct
ramshackel	ramshackle	ratchitt	ratchet
rancker	rancor	ratcio	ratio
randem	random	rathskellar	rathskeller
randsom	ransom	rationelize	rationalize
rangle	wrangle	rationnal	rationale
rankel	rankle	ratskeller	rathskeller
ransac	ransack	rattify	ratify
ransid	rancid	raviolli	ravioli
ranuculous	ranunculus	ravvage	ravage
rapchure	rapture	ravvel	ravel
rapell	rappel	ravvenous	ravenous
rappasity	rapacity	ravvin	raven
rappascious	rapacious	rawcus	raucous
rapperian	riparian	rawnchy	raunchy
rappid	rapid	Ray's syndrome	Reye's syndrome
rappor	rapport	raydome	radome
rapproachmont	rapprochement	raydon	radon
rappsodize	rhapsodize	Raynawd's disease	Raynaud's disease
rappsody	rhapsody		
rapscalleon	rapscallion	rayzor	razor
rapter	raptor	razorial	rasorial
raptoreal	raptorial	razzberry	raspberry
rapyer	rapier	reack	wrack
raquett	racket	reactavate	reactivate
raquett	racquet	reacter	reactor
rarrify	rarefy	readally	readily
rarrity	rarity	reajent	reagent
rasberry	raspberry	reak	reek (smell)
rascule	rascal	reak	wreak (to make something happen)
rashiocination	ratiocination		
rason de etre	raison d'être		
rassp	rasp	realline	realign
Rastafarrean	Rastafarian	reallistic	realistic
ratan	rattan	reatta	riata

Incorrect	Correct	Incorrect	Correct
rebbel	rebel	recoop	recoup
rebbellion	rebellion	recoose	recuse
rebuf	rebuff	recreasion	recreation
rebutt	rebut	recroot	recruit
rebuttle	rebuttal	recrudessence	recrudescence
recalcitrent	recalcitrant	rectanguler	rectangular
recappitulate	recapitulate	rectatude	rectitude
reccommend	recommend	rectem	rectum
recconize	recognize	recter	rector
recconoiter	reconnoiter	rectifie	rectify
receeded	recede	rectorry	rectory
receit	receipt	recundite	recondite
recepsion	reception	recupperate	recuperate
receptical	receptacle	recurranse	recurrence
recescion	recession	recusent	recusant
rech	retch	reddily	readily
rechersha	recherche	reddolent	redolent
recieve	receive	redduction	reduction
recipie	recipe	redempsion	redemption
recippient	recipient	redevivus	redivivus
reciproccal	reciprocal	redgement	regiment
reciproccate	reciprocate	recteo ad absurdem	reductio ad absurdum
reciprositty	reciprocity	redundensy	redundancy
recklamation	reclamation	redundent	redundant
reclame	reclaim	reegal	regal
reclemation	reclamation	reele	real (actual)
recloose	recluse	reele	reel (spool)
recognazanse	recognizance	reelizasion	realization
recompence	recompense	reemburse	reimburse
reconnasance	reconnaissance	reesling	Riesling
reconsile	reconcile	reeson	reason
reconsilliasion	reconciliation	reetail	retail
reconsillyatory	reconciliatory	reetorical	rhetorical
recoo	recoup		

Incorrect	Correct	Incorrect	Correct
refaree	referee	regulatorry	regulatory
refectary	refectory	regurjatate	regurgitate
referbish	refurbish	rehabillatate	rehabilitate
refferal	referral	rehersel	rehearsal
refferee	referee	reigne	reign
refferendum	referendum	reinne	rein
reffuge	refuge	reiterrate	reiterate
reffugee	refugee	rejuvinate	rejuvenate
reflecsive	reflexive	rekant	recant
reflecter	reflector	relapps	relapse
reflucks	reflux	relativaty	relativity
reformitory	reformatory	relativizm	relativism
refracsion	refraction	relator	realtor
refractary	refractory	relaxasion	relaxation
refrane	refrain	relecsion	reflection
refrigerater	refrigerator	releef	relief
refrigerrent	refrigerant	releese	release
refullgent	refulgent	releeve	relieve
refuzal	refusal	relenquish	relinquish
regail	regale	reletive	relative
regallia	regalia	reliabel	reliable
Regan	Reagan (president)	relience	reliance
		religeon	religion
regincy	regency	religeous	religious
regeon	region	relint	relent
reggay	reggae	rellagate	relegate
reggicide	regicide	rellavant	relevant
reggiman	regimen	rellic	relic
reggistrar	registrar	rellish	relish
reggular	regular	relm	realm
regotta	regatta	reluctence	reluctance
regresion	regression	reluctent	reluctant
regrettible	regrettable	remane	remain
regulasion	regulation	remarkible	remarkable

Incorrect	Correct	Incorrect	Correct
Rembrant	Rembrandt	reorganizasion	reorganization
remeadiation	remediation	repartay	repartee
remedeal	remedial	repatriot	repatriate
remembrence	remembrance	repeil	repeal
reminesce	reminisce	repentence	repentance
remis	remiss	repentent	repentant
remisseon	remission	repercuscion	repercussion
remitt	remit	repient	repent
remittence	remittance	replacasion	replication
remmady	remedy	replacate	replicate
remmanesence	reminiscence	repleate	replete
remminiscent	reminiscent	replennish	replenish
remmonstrate	remonstrate	reposess	repossess
remnent	remnant	repossed	repose
remorce	remorse	repossitory	repository
remorra	remora	repparation	reparation
remotelly	remotely	reppatition	repetition
removval	removal	reppel	repel
remunerration	remuneration	reppellant	repellent
renasence	renascence	reppertore	repertoire
rendavous	rendezvous	reppertory	repertory
rendission	rendition	repplica	replica
renig	renege (go back on a promise)	reppramand	reprimand
		repprobait	reprobate
Renn	Rennes (French city)	repputable	reputable
		repputation	reputation
rennagade	renegade	reppute	repute
rennal	renal	reprasentative	representative
rennasance	renaissance	repreeve	reprieve
renouned	renowned	reprehensable	reprehensible
renounse	renounce	representasion	representation
rentel	rental	represseon	repression
rentgun	roentgen	reprisle	reprisal
Reo di janero	Rio de Janeiro	reproch	reproach

Incorrect	Correct	Incorrect	Correct
reptiel	reptile	respratory	respiratory
republacan	republican	ressadue	residue
repugnent	repugnant	ressalute	resolute
repullsive	repulsive	ressatation	recitation
repulscion	repulsion	resscue	rescue
requassit	requisite	resservation	reservation
requier	require	ressidence	residence
requiescet	requiescat	ressidential	residential
requiremint	requirement	ressignation	resignation
requissition	requisition	ressin	resin
requium	requiem	ressle	wrestle
rescend	rescind	ressonent	resonant
rescent	recent	resspit	respite
rescently	recently	resstive	restive
rescisseon	rescission	restarateur	restaurateur
resemblence	resemblance	restatution	restitution
reservoer	reservoir	restorration	restoration
reshuffel	reshuffle	restorrative	restorative
residant	resident	restrane	restrain
residdavism	recidivism	restreint	restraint
resilliance	resilience	restricsion	restriction
resistence	resistance	restruant	restaurant
resonence	resonance	restruckure	restructure
resonnator	resonator	resultent	resultant
respectfull	respectful	resurjent	resurgent
respectibillaty	respectability	resussitate	resuscitate
respectible	respectable	retainner	retainer
respirrater	respirator	retalliate	retaliate
respirration	respiration	retardent	retardant
resplendint	resplendent	retension	retention
responce	response	retentave	retentive
respondant	respondent	retinapathy	retinopathy
responscive	responsive	retrabution	retribution
responsibillaty	responsibility	retract	retract

Incorrect	Correct	Incorrect	Correct
retractible	retractable	revitallize	revitalize
retrafit	retrofit	revivel	revival
retraspective	retrospective	revocabel	revocable
retred	retread	revolutionery	revolutionary
retreet	retreat	revulzion	revulsion
retreeve	retrieve	revvalee	reveille
retreval	retrieval	revvalution	revolution
retrinch	retrench	revvanue	revenue
retrospecsion	retrospection	revvanuer	revenuer
retroviris	retrovirus	revvel	revel
retsena	retsina	revvelation	revelation
rettaric	rhetoric	revverend	reverend
rettasence	reticence	revvery	revery
retticent	reticent	rezent	resent
rettina	retina	rezidual	residual
rettinue	retinue	rezist	resist
rettroactive	retroactive	rezistance	resistance
reunnion	reunion	rezolve	resolve
reveel	reveal	rezort	resort
reveer	revere	rezound	resound
revelie	reveille	rezume	resume
revennant	revenant	rezumption	resumption
reverbarate	reverberate	rezurrection	resurrection
reverense	reverence	rezzin	resin
reverie	revery	rhapsaddy	rhapsody
reverrent	reverent	rheeastat	rheostat
reversable	reversible	rheeomater	rheometer
reversel	reversal	rhessus	rhesus
reverseon	reversion	rheumatizm	rheumatism
reveu	revue	rhime	rhyme
reviel	revile	rhinaplasty	rhinoplasty
revinge	revenge	Rhinish	Rhenish
revirt	revert	rhinocerras	rhinoceros
revission	revision	rhoddadendren	rhododendron

Incorrect	Correct	Incorrect	Correct
riat	rite (ritual)	ripost	riposte
riatous	riotous	ripp rapp	riprap
ribbald	ribald	rippel	ripple
ribboflavin	riboflavin	ripudiate	repudiate
ribonucliec	ribonucleic	riskey	risky (dangerous)
rickashay	ricochet	risquay	risqué (suggestive)
rickitts	rickets		
rickoshay	richochet	rissotto	risotto
rickotta	ricotta	rist	wrist
Rickter scale	Richter scale	rittuel	ritual
ricktus	rictus	rivalerous	rivalrous
riddact	redact	rivelry	rivalry
riddacule	ridicule	rivle	rival
riddeem	redeem	rivvet	rivet
riddence	riddance	rivvulet	rivulet
riddiculus	ridiculous	rizzable	risible
ridress	redress	Roads scholar	Rhodes scholar
rie	rye (grain)	roal	role (character), roll (list)
rie	wry (crooked)		
riet	right	roal model	role model
riet	rite	roame	roam (wander)
rifel	rifle	roat	rote
riggamaroll	rigmarole	robbin	robin
riggatony	rigatoni	robbotic	robotic
riggid	rigid	robbottics	robotics
riggidity	rigidity	roche	roach
riggle	wriggle	rococco	rococo
riggor	rigor	rodant	rodent
riggor mortiss	rigor mortis	rodayo	rodeo
riggorous	rigorous	rodora	rhodora
rightous	righteous	roebott	robot
rinestone	rhinestone	Roem	Rome (city)
rinovirus	rhinovirus	rogge	rogue
riparrean	riparian	Rokefurt	Roquefort

Incorrect	Correct	Incorrect	Correct
Rollfing	Rolfing	rottund	rotund
romain	romaine	Rotwiler	Rottweiler
romantacism	romanticism	roude	rood (a cross)
romboid	rhomboid	roude	rude (impolite)
rombus	rhombus	roudy	rowdy
Romio	Romeo	roufuss	rufous
Rommany	Romany	roullet	roulette
rondavou	rendezvous	roundallay	roundelay
roo	roux (flour and fat)	roundell	roundel
		roustabbout	roustabout
roo	rue (regret)	routeen	routine
roode	rood (a cross)	routter	router
roode	rude	rouze	rouse
roofean	ruffian	rowall	rowel
rooje	rouge	rowe	row (use oars)
roomalade	roumalade	rowe	row (spat)
roomatoid	rheumatoid	rowst	roust
roon	rune	rowt	rout
roonick	runic	rowt	route
roopea	rupee	royellty	royalty
rootabaga	rutabaga	rozery	rosary
roote	route	rozett	rosette
roothless	ruthless	Rozetta stone	Rosetta stone
Rorshock	Rorschach	ruay	roué
Rossacrucian	Rosicrucian	rubbel	rubble
rossin	rosin	rubbella	rubella
rosster	roster	rubbesh	rubbish
rosstrum	rostrum	rubell	ruble
rotagraveur	rotogravure	Rubinesque	Rubenesque
rotater	rotator	Rubiyatt	Rubaiyat
roter	rotor	rubrick	rubric
Roterian	Rotarian	rucuss	ruckus
rotissary	rotisserie	rudament	rudiment
rottary	rotary	rudamentery	rudimentary

Incorrect	Correct	Incorrect	Correct
ruddar	rudder	rummije	rummage
ruebarb	rhubarb	rumpass	rumpus
ruebin	reuben	rumpel	rumple
ruffe	rough	Rumplestiltsken	Rumpelstiltskin
ruffien	ruffian	runcibel	runcible
ruinacion	ruination	runnaway	runaway
ruinnus	ruinous	rupsure	rupture
rumbel	rumble	rurrel	rural
rumer	rumor	russitt	russet
rumin	rumen	russle	rustle
ruminnant	ruminant	rustick	rustic
ruminnate	ruminate	rythym	rhythm
rummbah	rumba	rythymical	rhythmical

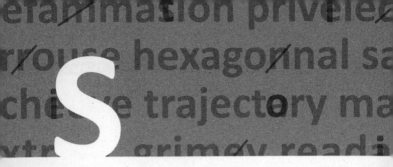

Most Commonly Misspelled Words

- sacrifice
- scissors
- separate
- similar
- sincerely
- soldier
- strengthen
- succeed
- successfully
- surprise

Incorrect	Correct	Incorrect	Correct
sabbatage	sabotage	saffrin	saffron
sabbatarrian	sabbatarian	sagga	saga
sabbaticle	sabbatical	saggacity	sagacity
sabbature	saboteur	saggo	sago
sabber	saber	Sagittareus	Sagittarius
Sabbeth	Sabbath	sagoe	sago (palm, starch)
sabbo	sabot		
sabel	sable	sagoe	sego (lily)
Sacajawea	Sacagawea	Saharra	Sahara
sacbutt	sackbut	saheeb	sahib
saccad	saccade	sahn	sans
saccarine	saccharin (sweetner), saccharine (sweet)	sahn souci	sans souci
		saicred	sacred
		saik	sake (benefit)
		sailler	sailor
saccroilliac	sacroiliac	saky	sake (drink)
sachell	satchel	salam	salaam
sackrosanct	sacrosanct	salamagundi	salmagundi
sacrafice	sacrifice	saliant	salient
sacrafishial	sacrificial	salevary	salivary
sacrelige	sacrilege	sallable	salable
sacrement	sacrament	sallacious	salacious
sacristan	sacristan	sallam	salaam
saddhu	sadhu	sallamander	salamander
saddiron	sadiron	sallamy	salami
saddism	sadism	sallan	salon
saddomassachism	sadomasochism	sallary	salary
sael	sail (boating)	sallicylic acid	salicylic acid
sael	sale (exchange money for goods)	salline	saline
		Sallisberry steak	Salisbury steak
saen	sane	salliva	saliva
saffire	sapphire	sallivate	salivate
safflour	safflower	sallo	sallow
Saffo	Sappho	Sallomi	Salome

Incorrect	Correct	Incorrect	Correct
salloon	saloon	sandel	sandal
sallsa	salsa	sanderrac	sandarac
sallubrious	salubrious	sandpapper	sandpaper
sallutary	salutary	sandwitch	sandwich
sallutation	salutation	sangreea	sangria
sallute	salute	sangwine	sanguine
sallver	salver	sangwinery	sanguinary
sallvo	salvo	sanitareum	sanatorium
saltattory	saltatory	sanne	seine
saltery	psaltery	sannitarian	sanitarian
saltpetter	saltpeter	sannitation	sanitation
saltumbocca	saltimbocca	sannitery	sanitary
saluditorian	salutatorian	sannitoreum	sanatorium
salvacion	salvation	sannity	sanity
salvagable	salvageable	san-serrif	sans-serif
salvige	salvage	Sanskritt	Sanskrit
sambucca	sambuca	sant	saint
sambuh	samba	santhood	sainthood
samisdat	samizdat	sanwitch	sandwich
Sammaritan	Samaritan	sappid	sapid
sammisan	samisen	sappient	sapient
Sammoa	Samoa	sapprophite	saprophyte
sammon	salmon	saragraph	serigraph
sammovar	samovar	Sarahayvo	Sarajevo
sammurai	samurai	sarcastick	sarcastic
samonnella	salmonella	sarcazm	sarcasm
sampann	sampan	sarcofagus	sarcophagus
sanchion	sanction	sarcomma	sarcoma
sanctamonious	sanctimonious	sardeen	sardine
sanctaty	sanctity	sardonics	sardonyx
sanctiffy	sanctify	sardonnic	sardonic
sanctom	sanctum	sargassim	sargassum
sanctuery	sanctuary	sargeant	sergeant
san-cullote	sans-culotte	sarr	czar, tsar

Incorrect	Correct	Incorrect	Correct
Sarrasota	Sarasota	sautay	sauté
Sarratoga	Saratoga	sauvinnon blonc	sauvignon blanc
sarrong	sarong	savagry	savagery
sarry	sari	savaloy	saveloy
sarsenet	sarcenet	savery	savory
sarsperrila	sarsaparilla	savije	savage
sartoreal	sartorial	Saville	Seville
sasafrass	sassafras	savvana	savannah or savanna
sashem	sachem		
sashiate	satiate	savver	savor
sashimmi	sashimi	savvie	savvy
sasserdotal	sacerdotal	savwair faire	savoir faire
sasshay	sachet (perfume)	savyer	savior
sasshay	sashay (strut)	sawna	sauna
sassifras	sassafras	sawsage	sausage
sassquach	sasquatch	sawterne	sauterne
satallite	satellite	saxafrage	saxifrage
satannic	satanic	saxaphone	saxophone
satirracle	satirical	sayance	seance
satiyeasus	satyriasis	sayonnara	sayonara
satternalean	saturnalian	sayter	satyr
sattin	satin	saytrap	satrap
sattire	satire	scabberd	scabbard
sattisfactory	satisfactory	scabbies	scabies
satto voche	sotto voce	scabbrus	scabrous
sattori	satori	scaffeld	scaffold
satturate	saturate	scafflaw	scofflaw
Satturnalia	Saturnalia	scaleen	scalene
satturnine	saturnine	scaley	scaly
saucey	saucy	scallawag	scalawag
Saudia Arabia	Saudi Arabia	scalleon	scallion
saugarro	saguaro	scallopinni	scaloppine
saunna	sauna	scallup	scallop
saussaly	saucily	scampy	scampi

Incorrect	Correct	Incorrect	Correct
scandallize	scandalize	scialism	sciolism
scandallous	scandalous	sciattic	sciatic
scandel	scandal	sciattica	sciatica
Scandinavvian	Scandinavian	scientiffic	scientific
scanseon	scansion	scimmatar	scimitar
scantey	scanty	scione	scion
scapegote	scapegoat	scissers	scissors
scappel	scalpel	scithe	scythe
scapulla	scapula	scleromma	scleroma
scarafy	scarify	sclerossis	sclerosis
scarff	scarf	sclerottic	sclerotic
scarletina	scarlatina	sclerra	sclera
scarrab	scarab	scoan	scone
scarse	scarce	scolleosis	scoliosis
scattalogical	scatological	sconse	sconce
scaur	scour	scootum	scutum
scaut	scout	scopolameen	scopolamine
scavanger	scavenger	scorche	scorch
scaylar	scalar	scornfull	scornful
sceenic	scenic	Scorpeo	Scorpio
scenarrio	scenario	scorpian	scorpion
sceptar	scepter	scotsch	scotch
sceptic	skeptic	scott-free	scot-free
scheduel	schedule	scoundral	scoundrel
scheem	scheme	scrabbil	scrabble
Schenectedy	Schenectady	scrambel	scramble
Scherrazade	Scheherazade	scrappel	scrapple
schizofrenia	schizophrenia	scraul	scrawl
schoddenfreude	schadenfreude	scraunge	scrounge
scholiest	scholiast	scrauny	scrawny
schollarly	scholarly	scread	screed
schollastic	scholastic	screetch	screech
schrewd	shrewd	scremp	scrimp
schwau	schwa	scremshaw	scrimshaw

Incorrect	Correct	Incorrect	Correct
scribbel	scribble	secondery	secondary
scripshure	scripture	secoure	secure
scrivvener	scrivener	secracy	secrecy
scrodd	scrod	secratariat	secretariat
scroff	scruff	secreet	secrete
scroffulous	scrofulous	secter	sector
scrole	scroll	secterrian	sectarian
scrotem	scrotum	secularizm	secularism
scrumpsious	scrumptious	seculer	secular
scrupples	scruples	secum	cecum
scrupullous	scrupulous	seddan	sedan
scrutanize	scrutinize	seddate	sedate
scrutanny	scrutiny	seddative	sedative
scubba	scuba	seddentary	sedentary
scuffel	scuffle	Sedder	Seder
sculk	skulk	seddition	sedition
scullary	scullery	sedduce	seduce
sculle	scull (oar)	sedduction	seduction
sculleon	scullion	seddulus	sedulous
sculpter	sculptor	seecant	secant
scurge	scourge	seecrative	secretive
scurrylous	scurrilous	seedum	sedum
scurvey	scurvy	Seekh	Sikh (sect)
scutchion	scutcheon	seelacanth	coelacanth
scuttel	scuttle	seelia	cilia
scuttelbut	scuttlebutt	seelocanth	coelacanth
Seallab	Sealab	seemen	semen
sealocanth	coelacanth	seemley	seemly
seamenship	seamanship	seeple	sepal
seathe	seethe	seequell	sequel
sebacious	sebaceous	seeqwin	sequin
sebbarhea	seborrhea	seersuccer	seersucker
seccatures	secateurs	seeson	season
secludde	seclude	seet-see fly	tsetse fly

Incorrect	Correct	Incorrect	Correct
seeur	sewer	semmicolon	semicolon
sege	sedge	semmifinalist	semifinalist
segmant	segment	semminal	seminal
segnore	signore	semminarian	seminarian
segragate	segregate	Semminole	Seminole
seguero	saguaro	semmiotics	semiotics
segway	segue	semmipermeable	semipermeable
seige	siege	semmiprecious	semiprecious
seismagraph	seismograph	Semmitic	Semitic
seista	siesta	semper fidellis	semper fidelis
seisure	seizure	senascence	senescence
seive	sieve	seniorrity	seniority
sellabration	celebration	sennah	senna
sellafane	cellophane	sennat	sennit
selldom	seldom	sennator	senator
selle	sell	Senneca	Seneca
sellect	select	Sennegal	Senegal
sellenium	selenium	sennescense	senescence
sellfish	selfish	sennescent	senescent
selltzer	seltzer	sennile	senile
selluler	cellular	sensationallism	sensationalism
sellvage	selvage	sensative	sensitive
semantick	semantic	sensibillity	sensibility
semblence	semblance	sensient	sentient
sement	cement	sensimilla	sinsemilla
semiphore	semaphore	senssus	census
semmalina	semolina	sensuallity	sensuality
semmanary	seminary	sentament	sentiment
semmantics	semantics	sentimentel	sentimental
semmapermeable	semipermeable	sentinnel	sentinel
semmatery	cemetery	Sephardec	Sephardic
semmester	semester	sepparate	separate
semmi-annual	semiannual	sepparation	separation

Incorrect	Correct	Incorrect	Correct
seppsus	sepsis	serris	cirrus
sepptic	septic	serrum	serum
sepratist	separatist	servamechanism	servomechanism
septom	septum	servatude	servitude
septuagenarrian	septuagenarian	servent	servant
sepulchrel	sepulchral	servicable	serviceable
sepulchur	sepulcher	serviete	serviette
seqoyia	sequoia	serville	servile
sequestrasion	sequestration	sesession	secession
sequinse	sequence	sesquicentenneal	sesquicentennial
seraff	seraph	sesquipeddalean	sesquipedalian
sereen	serene	sessal	sessile
serendippity	serendipity	sessame	sesame
seriatem	seriatim	sessede	secede
serius	serious (grave)	sesspool	cesspool
serius	Sirius (star)	sestinna	sestina
serloin	sirloin	setee	settee
serman	sermon	setsee fly	tsetse fly
sermonnize	sermonize	settel	settle
serpant	serpent	seveer	severe
serpanteen	serpentine	seventene	seventeen
serralio	seraglio	seventeth	seventieth
serranade	serenade	severly	severely
serrape	serape	severrity	severity
serratonen	serotonin	sevvant	savant
serratted	serrated	sevveral	several
serreal	serial (sequence)	sevverence	severance
serrebrum	cerebrum	sexagessimal	sexagesimal
serrendippitus	serendipitous	sexollogy	sexology
serrendippity	serendipity	sextent	sextant
serries	series	sextupplet	sextuplet
serrif	serif	sexuel	sexual
serrious	serious	sfagnam	sphagnum

Incorrect	Correct	Incorrect	Correct
sfeer	sphere	Shannendoa	Shenandoah
sfincter	sphincter	shantoos	chanteuse
sfinx	sphinx	shapperone	chaperon (male)
sfortzando	sforzando		chaperone (female)
shackel	shackle		
shaddore	chador	shappoe	chapeau
Shadrack	Shadrach	Sharalay	Charolais
shaffon	chiffon	shardonnay	chardonnay
shagrin	chagrin	shardosh	czardas
Shakesperian	Shakespearean	sharoot	cheroot
shakko	shako	sharrade	charade
shalam	shalom	sharteuss	chartreuse
shallay	chalet	shattar	shatter
shalott	shallot	shatto	chateau
shambels	shambles	shattobriand	chateaubriand
shambollic	shambolic	shattoe	chateau
shambray	chambray	shaul	shawl
shamize	chemise	shaum	shawm
shammpoo	shampoo	Shaunee	Shawnee
shammy	chamois	Shavvean	Shavian
shamon	shaman	shearr	sheer
shampane	champagne	sheatsu	shiatsu
shamroc	shamrock	sheef	sheaf
shandalier	chandelier	sheek	chic (stylish)
shandygaff	shandygaff	sheek	sheik (chief)
shaneal	chenille	sheeld	shield
Shanghi	Shanghai (city)	sheerwater	shearwater
shanghi	shanghai (kidnap)	sheeth	sheath
		sheeves	sheaves
Shanghie	Shanghai (city)	shef	chef
shanghie	shanghai (kidnap)	Sheharizade	Scheherezade
		sheir	sheer
Shangra-Lah	Shangri-La	sheirs	shears
shanker	chancre	Sheite	Shiite

Incorrect	Correct	Incorrect	Correct
shekkel	shekel	shittum	shittim
shelack	shellac	shivalree	chivalry
shelldrake	sheldrake	shivaree	charivari
Shelltie	Sheltie	shivva	shiva
shem	shim	shlemiel	schlemiel
shene	sheen	shlep	schlep
Shentoism	Shintoism	shlepp	schlep
shenyon	chignon	shlockmaster	schlockmeister
shepard	shepherd	shmaltz	schmaltz
sherbert	sherbet	shmooze	schmooze
sherk	shirk	shnapps	schnapps
sherrif	sheriff	shnausser	schnauzer
shershay la fomme	cherchez la femme	shnitzel	schnitzel
		shnook	schnook
Shetlenn	Shetland	shoddenfroyde	schadenfreude
sheva	shiva	shoddey	shoddy
shevvaleer	chevalier	shoeng	shoeing
shewing	shoeing	shofer	chauffeur (driver), shofar (ram's horn)
Shiat Zu	Shih Tzu		
shiboleth	shibboleth		
shicksa	shiksa	shofur	chauffeur (driver), shofar (ram's horn)
shiek	sheik		
shiffarobe	chifforobe		
shillaley	shillelagh	shole	shoal
Shin Fane	Sinn Fein	shonson	chanson
shiney	shiny	Shopann	Chopin
shing	shingles	shortege	shortage
shinnen blank	chenin blanc	Shoshony	Shoshone
shin splits	shin splints	shote	shoat
shipreck	shipwreck	shotissish	schottische
shir	shirr	shoud	should
Shirpa	Sherpa	shovanism	chauvinism
shish kebbab	shish kebab	showgun	shogun
shitake	shiitake	shrapnell	shrapnel

Incorrect	Correct	Incorrect	Correct
shreek	shriek	siena	Siena (city)
shreft	shrift	siena	sienna (color)
shremp	shrimp	siera	sierra
shrenk	shrink	siet	site
shrille	shrill	sieze	seize
shrivvel	shrivel	sifer	cipher
shrou	shrew	sifon	siphon
shrowd	shroud	Sigfreed	Siegfried
shrubb	shrub	siggar	cigar
shrunkin	shrunken	siggarat	cigarette
shtik	shtick	siggma	sigma
shuffel	shuffle	siggnature	signature
shumac	sumac	sigmoidascope	sigmoidoscope
shuss	schuss	sigmoyd	sigmoid
shuttel	shuttle	Signai	Sinai
Shyanne	Cheyenne	signatorry	signatory
shycannery	chicanery	signett	signet
Shylo	Shiloh	signifficance	significance
shystir	shyster	silense	silence
Sibalius	Sibelius	Silla	Scylla
sibbilant	sibilant	sillable	syllable
sibbling	sibling	sillabus	syllabus
sibil	sibyl	sillacon	silicon (chemical element)
sibyline	sibylline		
siccada	cicada	sillacon	silicone (rubbery polymer)
siccamore	sycamore		
siccatris	cicatrix	sillacone	silicon (chemical element), silicone (rubbery polymer)
sichiatrist	psychiatrist		
sickel	sickle		
sickel cell anemia	sickle cell anemia		
sidder	siddur	sillege	silage
sidel	sidle	sillenderer	cylinder
sider	cider	sillica	silica
siderreal	sidereal	sillicosis	silicosis

Incorrect	Correct	Incorrect	Correct
silloette	silhouette	sinessence	senescence
silph	sylph	siney die	sine die
silvan	sylvan	siney qua non	sine qua non
silverculture	silviculture	sinfull	sinful
silverwear	silverware	Singalese	Singhalese
silvvavitz	slivovitz	singelton	singleton
Simarron	Cimarron	singuler	singular
simbiosis	symbiosis	sinje	singe
simbolize	symbolize	sinkfoil	cinquefoil
Simborska	Szymborska	sinkshur	cincture
Simese	Siamese	sinnamon	cinnamon
simmally	simile	sinnasure	cynosure
simmatry	symmetry	sinnecure	sinecure
simmian	simian	sinnergy	synergy
simmilarety	similarity	sinnew	sinew
simmiler	similar	sinnic	cynic
simmilitude	similitude	sinnister	sinister
simmpattico	simpatico	sinnuous	sinuous
simmulate	simulate	sinnus	sinus
simpathy	sympathy	sinnusitis	sinusitis
simpliffy	simplify	sinofile	sinophile
simplissaty	simplicity	sinser	censor (suppressor)
simplistick	simplistic		
simultanious	simultaneous	sinser	sensor (measuring device)
sinazoid	sinusoid		
sinceer	sincere		
sincerley	sincerely	sinser	censer (incense burner)
sincronicity	synchronicity		
sincronize	synchronize	sinsoreous	censorious
sincronous	synchronous	sintallate	scintillate
sinder	cinder	sintilla	scintilla
sindicate	syndicate	sion	scion
sindicated	syndicated	Siou	Sioux
sindrome	syndrome	sircharge	surcharge

Incorrect	Correct	Incorrect	Correct
sircle	circle	sittuation	situation
sircuits	circuits	sivvet	civet
sirculation	circulation	sivvies	civvies
sireen	siren	sixtyith	sixtieth
sirname	surname	sizeable	sizable
sirringe	syringe	sizemograph	seismograph
sirrocco	sirocco	sizemommatur	seismometer
sirrup	syrup	sizzim	schism
sirrus	cirrus	sizzmattic	schismatic
sirtax	surtax	skamp	scamp
sisken	siskin	skane	skein
sissel	scissile (metal)	skarp	scarp
sissel	sisal (plant, fiber)	skathing	scathing
		skeat	skeet
Sissero	Cicero	skedaddel	skedaddle
sissile	scissile (metal)	skegg	skeg
sissile	sisal (plant, fiber)	skeing	skiing
		skelton	skeleton
Sisstine	Sistine	skematic	schematic
Sissyphian	Sisyphean	skematize	schematize
Sissyphus	Sisyphus	skempy	skimpy
sist	cyst	skeptacism	skepticism
sistascope	cystoscope	skerl	skirl
Sisteen Chapel	Sistine Chapel	skertzando	scherzando
sistern	cistern	skertzo	scherzo
sitation	citation	skettles	skittles
sitric	citric	skiier	skier
sitsmark	sitzmark	skilfull	skillful
sittadale	citadel	skillit	skillet
sittar	sitar	skimp	scrimp
sittronella	citronella	skipperke	schipperke
sittrus	citrus	skirmesh	skirmish
sitts bath	sitz bath	skism	schism
sittuated	situated	skitzoid	schizoid

Incorrect	Correct	Incorrect	Correct
skitzophrenia	schizophrenia	slattarn	slattern
sklera	sclera	slauch	slouch
skleroma	scleroma	slauter	slaughter
sklerosis	sclerosis	slaverry	slavery
sklerottic	sclerotic	slavofile	slavophile
skole	skoal	slavvish	slavish
skoliosis	scoliosis	slaye	slay (kill)
skonce	sconce	slaye	sleigh (sled)
skone	scone	sleak	sleek
skoolmarm	schoolmarm	sledghammar	sledgehammer
skooner	schooner	sleeze	sleaze
skorch	scorch	sleezy	sleazy
skrim	scrim	sleim	slime
skrimmidge	scrimmage	slenk	slink
skrimshau	scrimshaw	sliegh	sleigh (sled)
skrod	scrod	slieght	slight
skroffulous	scrofulous	slight of hand	sleight of hand
skuba	scuba	slimey	slimy
skudding	scudding	slinder	slender
skuer	skewer	slipery	slippery
skullduggary	skullduggery	slite	slight
skullerry	scullery	slithir	slither
skulpt	sculpt	slober	slobber
skuppers	scuppers	slogen	slogan
skurge	scourge	sloo	slue
skurrilous	scurrilous	sloose	sluice
skuttlebutt	scuttlebutt	slosch	slosh
skuzzy	scuzzy	slouth	sloth
skwire	squire	sluff	slough
slagg	slag	sluge	sludge
slalam	slalom	sluggerd	sluggard
slandrous	slanderous	slumbar	slumber
slannder	slander	slupe	sloop
slathere	slather	slurrey	slurry

Incorrect	Correct	Incorrect	Correct
slusch	slush	snobbary	snobbery
sluth	sleuth	snoocker	snooker
sluvven	sloven	snoose	snooze
sluvvenly	slovenly	snorkle	snorkel
sluw	slew	snuggel	snuggle
smarmey	smarmy	snyde	snide
smatterring	smattering	soaber	sober
smealt	smelt	soal	sole (only, fish)
smeer	smear	soal	soul (spirit)
smerk	smirk	soare	soar
smidgin	smidgen	sobriaty	sobriety
smillax	smilax	sobriquay	sobriquet
smithareens	smithereens	socal	socle
Smithsonean	Smithsonian	Soccar torte	Sacher torte
smokey	smoky	socciable	sociable
smoldir	smolder	socialise	socialize
Smollet	Smollett	socializm	socialism
smorgusboard	smorgasbord	sociapath	sociopath
smuge	smudge	sociaty	society
smuther	smother	sociolingwistics	sociolinguistics
snach	snatch	socky	sake (drink)
snaffu	snafu	Socrites	Socrates
snair	snare	sodallity	sodality
snairl	snarl	soddamy	sodomy
snale	snail	soddar	solder
snapdraggon	snapdragon	soddomize	sodomize
snear	sneer	soer	soar (fly)
sneek	sneak	soer	sore (pain)
sneiper	sniper	soffist	sophist
sniche	snitch	soffisticated	sophisticated
sniffels	sniffles	soffistication	sophistication
snikker	snicker	soffistry	sophistry
snikkersnee	snickersnee	softig	zaftig or zoftig
snippit	snippet	softwear	software

Incorrect	Correct	Incorrect	Correct
soirray	soiree	somnambullate	somnambulate
sojurne	sojourn	somnambullist	somnambulist
sokkey	sake (drink)	somnifarous	somniferous
solanoid	solenoid	song-frwah	sang-froid
solarrium	solarium	sonnar	sonar
soldiar	soldier	sonnata	sonata
soler	solar	sonnic	sonic
solfegio	solfeggio	sonnit	sonnet
solilloquy	soliloquy	sonnobouy	sonobuoy
sollace	solace	sonnogram	sonogram
sollacism	solecism	sonnorous	sonorous
sollarium	solarium	soodonym	pseudonym
sollely	solely	Sookote	Sukkot, Sukkoth
sollicit	solicit	Soony	Sunni
solliciter	solicitor	sooshi	sushi
sollicitus	solicitous	sophamore	sophomore
sollidarity	solidarity	sophistacated	sophisticated
sollidus	solidus	sophistacation	sophistication
sollipsizm	solipsism	soporrific	soporific
sollitare	solitaire	sorbit	sorbet
sollitery	solitary	Sorbone	Sorbonne
sollitude	solitude	sorcerry	sorcery
sollution	solution	sord	sword
soloman	Solomon	sorded	sordid
solstus	solstice	sorell	sorrel
solum	solemn	sorgum	sorghum
solvancy	solvency	soriasis	psoriasis
solvant	solvent	soritees	sorites
sombar	somber	sorrority	sorority
sombrerro	sombrero	sortaledge	sortilege
someleay	sommelier	sorty	sortie
sommatic	somatic	souce	souse
sommersault	somersault	souchef	sous-chef
somnalent	somnolent	soue	sou (money)

Incorrect	Correct	Incorrect	Correct
soue	sough (sound)	spastick	spastic
soufflay	souffle	spatulla	spatula
souh	sou (money)	spaun	spawn
souh	sough (sound)	spazm	spasm
soule	soul	speccialty	specialty
sounter	saunter	specculate	speculate
soup de jour	soup du jour	specculative	speculative
sourbraten	sauerbraten	speciallize	specialize
sourdoe	sourdough	specifficaly	specifically
sourkrout	sauerkraut	speciffication	specification
souterne	sauterne	speciman	specimen
souvlakkea	souvlakia	spek	spec ("on spec"), speck (bit)
soverein	sovereign		
sowe	sew (stitch)	spectacullar	spectacular
sowe	sow (seed)	spectater	spectator
soyouz	soyuz	spectram	spectrum
spaceal	spacial	spectrascope	spectroscope
spaceous	spacious	speelunker	spelunker
spaciel	spatial	spenster	spinster
spacific	specific	spermacide	spermicide
spackel	spackle	spermatazoa	spermatozoa
spagetti	spaghetti	spern	spurn
spaid	spayed	speshies	species
Spainyard	Spaniard	speshious	specious
spakkle	spackle	spevened	spavined
spanecopita	spanakopita	sphagnim	sphagnum
spangel	spangle	spheer	sphere
Spanglesh	Spanglish	sphenx	sphinx
sparce	sparse	sphericle	spherical
sparkleng	sparkling	sphygmomannometer	
sparten	spartan		sphygmomanometer
spashcock	spatchcock	spicket	spigot
spasial	spatial	spiderwart	spiderwort

Incorrect	Correct	Incorrect	Correct
spiggot	spigot	spreckstimme	sprechstimme
spina biffida	spina bifida	sprinkel	sprinkle
spinette	spinet	spritser	spritzer
spinnach	spinach	spue	spew
spinnaret	spinneret	spummony	spumoni
spinnet	spinet	spunge	sponge
spinniker	spinnaker	sputem	sputum
spinstir	spinster	sqaub	squab
spinthrift	spendthrift	squabbel	squabble
spiralkete	spirochete	squadren	squadron
spirel	spiral	squallid	squalid
spirituel	spiritual	squallor	squalor
spirrogira	spirogyra	squamus	squamous
spitoon	spittoon	squandor	squander
splean	spleen	squeejee	squeegee
splender	splendor	squeek	squeak
splent	splint	squeel	squeal
splenter	splinter	squeemish	squeamish
splinded	splendid	squelsh	squelch
splise	splice	squent	squint
spoliage	spoilage	squirell	squirrel
spondalosis	spondylosis	sqwad	squad
spondy	spondee	sqwid	squid
sponser	sponsor	sqwirm	squirm
spontanious	spontaneous	sqwirt	squirt
spontenaity	spontaneity	staaph	staph
spoonarism	spoonerism	stabelize	stabilize
spoorious	spurious	stabilety	stability
sporradic	sporadic	stacatto	staccato
sporren	sporran	stadeum	stadium
spouce	spouse	stafalocockus	staphylococcus
spraddel	spraddle	staffe	staff (stick, or employees)
spraul	sprawl		

Incorrect	Correct	Incorrect	Correct
staffe	staph (bacteria)	staylog	stalag
stagnent	stagnant	steak tartar	steak tartare
stallactite	stalactite	steake	stake (support post)
stallagmite	stalagmite		
staman	stamen	steake	steak (meat)
staminna	stamina	stealthe	stealth
stampeed	stampede	steant	stent (tube)
standerd	standard	steant	stint (time, save)
standerdise	standardize	steddy	steady
Stanislavski	Stanislavsky	steeley	steely
stanse	stance	steepal	steeple
stanshion	stanchion	steere	steer (direct)
stanzia	stanza	steere	stere (unit of measurement)
stapel	staple		
starbord	starboard	steeroid	steroid
starleng	starling	stefanotus	stephanotis
startel	startle	Steiglitz	Stieglitz
starteling	startling	steil	steal (rob)
stary	starry	steil	steel (metal)
stassis	stasis	steller	stellar
stationnery	stationary (unmoving)	stelthy	stealthy
		stensel	stencil
stationerry	stationery (paper)	stepps	steppes
		stereoptacon	stereopticon
stattic	static	sterleng	sterling
stattistics	statistics	sternam	sternum
statuery	statuary	sterreofonic	stereophonic
statuett	statuette	sterrile	sterile
stattus	statice (plant), status (situation)	sterrilize	sterilize
		sterrotype	stereotype
statutorry	statutory	stethascope	stethoscope
statutte	statute	stevadore	stevedore
stawnch	staunch	stewerd	steward

Incorrect	Correct	Incorrect	Correct
sticklar	stickler	stowt	stout
stickomythia	stichomythia	strabizmus	strabismus
stie	sty	straddel	straddle
stiffle	stifle	Stradivarious	Stradivarius
stigean	stygian	straggel	straggle
stigmattize	stigmatize	straightjacket	straitjacket
stigmuh	stigma	straight-laced	strait-laced
stilleto	stiletto	straite	straight
stimie	stymie	strangel	strangle
stimmulus	stimulus	stranguery	strangury
stimulent	stimulant	strangullation	strangulation
stine	stein	Strasburg	Strasberg (director)
Stineway	Steinway		
stingey	slingy	Strasburg	Strasbourg (city)
stipand	stipend	stratasphere	stratosphere
stipptic	styptic	strate	strait
stirup	stirrup	strattafication	stratification
Stix	Styx	strattagem	stratagem
stoaway	stowaway	strattegic	strategic
stodgey	stodgy	strattum	stratum
stoggie	stogie	strattus	stratus
stoiccal	stoical	Straus	Strauss
stoik	stoic	strech	stretch
stoisizm	stoicism	streek	streak
stokastic	stochastic	strenthen	strengthen
stolan	stolen	strepp	strep
stollan	stollen (bread)	streptacoccus	streptococcus
stommich	stomach	striatted	striated
Stonehinge	Stonehenge	stricknine	strychnine
stoney	stony	stridant	strident
storm and drang	Sturm und Drang	strinjent	stringent
storrage	storage	strinuous	strenuous
stote	stoat	strippling	stripling

Incorrect	Correct	Incorrect	Correct
Strivinsky	Stravinsky	sublimmate	sublimate
strobiscope	stroboscope	sublimminal	subliminal
strofe	strophe	submurge	submerge
strogannof	stroganoff	subordinnate	subordinate
stronshium	strontium	subordinnation	subordination
stroosel	streusel	subpena	subpoena
struchure	structure	subrett	soubrette
structurel	structural	subsadize	subsidize
struggel	struggle	subscripcion	subscription
stryated	striated	subserviant	subservient
stubbel	stubble	subsiddiary	subsidiary
stubburn	stubborn	subsistance	subsistence
stucko	stucco	subssiddy	subsidy
studeous	studious	substancial	substantial
stulltify	stultify	substanciate	substantiate
stupafacient	stupefacient	substatute	substitute
stupiddity	stupidity	substints	substance
stupify	stupefy	substratta	substrata
stuppendus	stupendous	subterfouge	subterfuge
stuppor	stupor	subterranian	subterranean
sturgion	sturgeon	subverzion	subversion
styalize	stylize	succatash	succotash
styllus	stylus	succede	succeed
subborn	suborn	succer	succor
subburban	suburban	success destime	succes d'estime
subburbia	suburbia	successer	successor
subconsious	subconscious	succsion	suction
subcutanious	subcutaneous	succum	succumb
subdivvision	subdivision	suchef	sous-chef
subdo	subdue	sucksess	success
subdomminant	subdominant	sucksessfully	successfully
subjuggate	subjugate	sucsession	succession
subjunktive	subjunctive	sucsinct	succinct

Incorrect	Correct	Incorrect	Correct
sucuestter	sequester	sundie	Sunday (day)
sucullent	succulent	sundreys	sundries
suddin	sudden	sundrie	sundry
suelter	swelter	sunommi	tsunami
suerve	swerve	superanuated	superannuated
sueveneer	souvenir	superceed	supersede
sufference	sufferance	supercillious	supercilious
suffise	suffice	supererrogatery	supererogatory
suffishent	sufficient	superfissial	superficial
suffrege	suffrage	superflous	superfluous
suffucate	suffocate	superintendant	superintendent
suffuze	suffuse	superiorrity	superiority
sugjest	suggest	superlettive	superlative
suiside	suicide	supernel	supernal
suitible	suitable	supernumerrary	supernumerary
suittor	suitor	supersaturrated	supersaturated
suk	souk	supersonick	supersonic
sukiyakki	sukiyaki	supersticious	superstitious
sukkatash	succotash	superstision	superstition
sulfer	sulfur	superviser	supervisor
sullan	sullen	suppine	supine
sullfite	sulfite	supplacate	supplicate
sultanna	sultana	supplecant	supplicant
sultrey	sultry	supplementery	supplementary
sumach	sumac	suppositorry	suppository
summa cum lawde	summa cum laude	suppusition	supposition
		suprano	soprano
summens	summons	supremmacy	supremacy
summet	summit	supression	suppression
summiry	summary	suprise	surprise
summulacrum	simulacrum	supurb	superb
sumptious	sumptuous	sureal	surreal
sundie	sundae (food)	sureptitious	surreptitious

Incorrect	Correct	Incorrect	Correct
suretty	surety	swade	suede
surfit	surfeit	swaggar	swagger
surggery	surgery	Swaheeli	Swahili
surgicle	surgical	swaink	swank
surgion	surgeon	swairthy	swarthy
surje	serge (cloth)	swammi	swami
surje	surge (swell)	sware	swear
surmize	surmise	swastaka	swastika
surpliss	surplice	swaushbuckling	swashbuckling
surragate	surrogate	swave	suave
surrepticious	surreptitious	swee generous	sui generis
surrge	surge (swell)	Sweedish	Swedish
surrosis	cirrhosis	swerl	swirl
sursingle	surcingle	swimmerette	swimmeret
survallence	surveillance	swindel	swindle
survivel	survival	switche	switch
susceptable	susceptible	swite	suite
sushe	sushi	swivil	swivel
suspencion	suspension	swizzel	swizzle
suspind	suspend	swoth	swath
suspission	suspicion	sybarrite	sybarite
Susquahana	Susquehanna	sychadellic	psychedelic
sussaphone	sousaphone	sychofant	sycophant
sustane	sustain	syllagism	syllogism
sustenence	sustenance	symbal	symbol
suttle	subtle	symbiossis	symbiosis
suttlety	subtlety	symbollize	symbolize
sutture	suture	symetrical	symmetrical
suvelte	svelte	sympathettic	sympathetic
suvide	sous vide	symphany	symphony
suzeran	suzerain	symphonnic	symphonic
swach	swatch	symposeum	symposium
swaddeling	swaddling	symptommatic	symptomatic

Incorrect	Correct	Incorrect	Correct
synaggog	synagogue	synoppsis	synopsis
synapce	synapse	syntacks	syntax
syncopasion	syncopation	synthasize	synthesize
syncronicity	synchronicity	synthasizer	synthesizer
syncronize	synchronize	synthessis	synthesis
syncronous	synchronous	synthettic	synthetic
syncrotism	syncretism	syon	scion
syne	sine	syphlus	syphilis
synecdaky	synecdoche	syrinje	syringe
synnanym	synonym	systemmatic	systematic
synnergy	synergy	systemmic	systemic
synnod	synod	sythe	scythe
synonnymous	synonymous	syzagy	syzygy

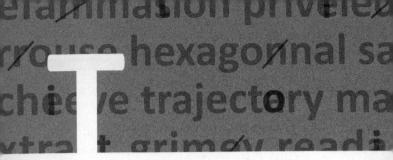

Most Commonly Misspelled Words

- talkative
- tangible
- taut
- technique
- temperature
- thorough
- through
- thumb
- truly
- twelfth

Incorrect	Correct	Incorrect	Correct
tabacco	tobacco	Tallmud	Talmud
tabard	tabbard	tallo	tallow
Tabbasco	Tabasco	tallon	talon
tabbernacle	tabernacle	tallus	talus
tabboo	taboo	tallyhoe	tallyho
tabbula rasa	tabula rasa	tamalee	tamale
tabbular	tabular	Tamanyism	Tammanyism
tabbulate	tabulate	tamarac	tamarack
tableture	tablature	tamborine	tambourine
tablow	tableau	tammarind	tamarind
tabloyd	tabloid	tammesis	tmesis
tachistascope	tachistoscope	tam-o-shantar	tam-o'-shanter
tackful	tactful	tampan	tampon
tackommater	tachometer	tandim	tandem
tackt	tact	tandury	tandoori
tacktics	tactics	tangello	tangelo
tackyarrhythmia	tachyarhythmia	tangencial	tangential
tackycardia	tachycardia	tangerrine	tangerine
taddpole	tadpole	tangint	tangent
taffita	taffeta	tangrum	tangram
Taggolog	Tagalog	Tanhouser	Tannhauser
tagliatele	tagliatelle	tanjible	tangible
tagmimics	tagmemics	tankerd	tankard
taheeni	tahini	tannager	tanager
Tahonno	Tejano	tannen	tannin
Taiwon	Taiwan	tant	taint
talck	talc	tantallize	tantalize
talegate	tailgate	tantemount	tantamount
talkathonn	talkathon	tantram	tantrum
talkitive	talkative	tao	tau
tallaria	talaria	tapiocca	tapioca
tallcum	talcum	tappas	tapas
tallent	talent	tappastry	tapestry
tallisman	talisman	tappir	tapir

Incorrect	Correct	Incorrect	Correct
tardygrade	tardigrade	tawdree	tawdry
tarmack	tarmac	tawney	tawny
tarmiggan	ptarmigan	tawt	taut
tarnesh	tarnish	taxadermy	taxidermy
tarpen	tarpon	tax deductable	tax deductible
tarpoline	tarpaulin	tax exxempt	tax exempt
tarrantula	tarantula	taxonnamy	taxonomy
tarre	tare	taylormade	tailor made
tarregon	tarragon	tay kwan doe	tae kwon do
tarrentella	tarantella	teathe	teethe
tarrif	tariff	teaze	tease
tarrn	tarn	teazel	teasel
tarro	taro (root)	technalogical	technological
tarro	tarot (card)	techneque	technique
tarsel	tarsal	technicallity	technicality
tarsiar	tarsier	technicle	technical
tarsis	tarsus	technission	technician
Tartarean	Tartarian	techtonnic	tectonic
tarten	tartan	teckniques	techniques
tarter	tartar	tedeous	tedious
tasell	tassel	tedeum	tedium
Tasmanean devil	Tasmanian devil	teejus	tedious
tassaturn	taciturn	teek	teak
tassit	tacit	Teekee	Tiki
tatoo	tattoo	teepea	tepee
tattami	tatami	teet	teat
tattardemalion	tatterdemalion	teetotel	teetotal
tattarsall	tattersall	teetter	teeter
tatteltale	tattletale	teil	teal
tattors	tatters	teim	teem
taup	taupe	teir	tier
Taurrus	Taurus	tektonic	tectonic
tautollogy	tautology	teliology	teleology
tavvern	tavern	tellagennic	telegenic

Incorrect	Correct	Incorrect	Correct
tellakinesis	telekinesis	tennacious	tenacious
tellamark	telemark	tennacity	tenacity
tellamarketing	telemarketing	tennacle	tentacle
tellascopic	telescopic	tennament	tenement
tellecommunication		tennant	tenant
	telecommunication	tennet	tenet
tellecommuting	telecommuting	tennon	tenon
tellematry	telemetry	tennuous	tenuous
tellepathy	telepathy	tensel	tinsel
telleportation	teleportation		(decoration)
tellesthesea	telesthesia	tensille	tensile (flexible)
telltell	telltale	tentlon	tension
Tellerium	Tellurium	tentirhooks	tenterhooks
tembler	temblor	tentitive	tentative
temerraty	temerity	tenyure	tenure
tempay	tempeh	teppid	tepid
temperence	temperance	tequilla	tequila
temperment	temperament	tercentennary	tercentenary
tempermintal	temperamental	tercit	tercet
temperra	tempera	terestreal	terrestrial
temporral	temporal	tergivversate	tergiversate
temporrary	temporary	termagunt	termagant
temporrize	temporize	termannater	terminator
temprature	temperature	termight	termite
tempurra	tempura	terminnal	terminal
tenasity	tenacity	terminnate	terminate
tendancy	tendency	terminnus	terminus
tendenteous	tendentious	terminollogy	terminology
tenderrloine	tenderloin	terpsicharean	terpsichorean
tendonnitis	tendinitis or	terra incogneto	terra incognita
	tendonitis	terrable	terrible
tendrill	tendril	terrah cottah	terra cotta
tener	tenor	terrah ferma	terra firma
tennable	tenable	terrareum	terrarium

Incorrect	Correct	Incorrect	Correct
terrepin	terrapin	thawng	thong
terrer	terror	theatrecal	theatrical
terrerist	terrorist	theeces	theses
terriffic	terrific	theef	thief
territorrial	territorial	theeism	theism
terriyakki	teriyaki	ther	their
terrodactal	pterodactyl		(possessive),
terrorise	terrorize		there (location),
terrorizm	terrorism		they're
terryaki	teriyaki		(contraction of
tertiarry	tertiary		"they are")
tertza rima	terza rima	theives	thieves
tesselate	tessellate	themattic	thematic
tesselated	tessellated	thenseforth	thenceforth
tesserackt	tesseract	theocrasy	theocracy
testamonial	testimonial	theoddolite	theodolite
testater	testator	theollogy	theology
testement	testament	theologean	theologian
testical	testicle	theomacky	theomachy
testosterrone	testosterone	theorettical	theoretical
tet-a-tet	tête-à-tête	theorrize	theorize
tethar	tether	theorum	theorem
tetnus	tetanus	theossafie	theosophy
tetrachlorride	tetrachloride	therabouts	thereabouts
tetrahedran	tetrahedron	therepy	therapy
tetzy fly	tsetse fly	therfore	therefore
textuer	texture	thermacline	thermocline
thach	thatch	thermacouple	thermocouple
thaen	thane	thermas	thermos
thalidommide	thalidomide	thermel	thermal
thallamus	thalamus	thermolumenescence	
thannatopsis	thanatopsis		thermoluminescence
thau	thaw	thermommater	thermometer
thawmaturgy	thaumaturgy	thermonucular	thermonuclear

Incorrect	Correct	Incorrect	Correct
therrabred	thoroughbred	throte	throat
therrapuetic	therapeutic	throtle	throttle
therteen	thirteen	throu	through
therupon	thereupon	thruout	throughout
thesaurous	thesaurus	thrusch	thrush
thibone	thighbone	thumm	thumb
thickenning	thickening	thurable	thurible
thiers	theirs	thurrifer	thurifer
thievary	thievery	thwert	thwart
thimbelfull	thimbleful	thyamine	thiamine
thimbul	thimble	thyroyd	thyroid
thime	thyme	tiarra	tiara
thirtyeth	thirtieth	tibbia	tibia
thistel	thistle	Tibettan	Tibetan
thonnic	chthonic	tichular	titular
thorrax	thorax	tickel	tickle
thorrou	thorough	tickelish	ticklish
thoughtfull	thoughtful	ticoon	tycoon
thoughtfullness	thoughtfulness	tiddaly winks	tiddlywinks
thoutfuly	thoughtfully	tidel	tidal
thowrn	thorn	tietration	titration
thraish	thrash	tiffeny	tiffany
threataned species	threatened species	tigresse	tigress (animal)
		Tigriss	Tigris (river)
thred	thread	tik	tic (spasm)
thredbare	threadbare	tik	tick (insect, clock sound)
thrennady	threnody		
threp	thrip	tillde	tilde
threshhold	threshold	tiloppia	tilapia
thrieve	thrive	timballe	timbale
thriftally	thriftily	timbar	timber (trees)
thriftey	thrifty	timbir	timbre (tone)
thrombosus	thrombosis	time immemmorial	time immemorial
throse	throes	time-lapps	time-lapse

Incorrect	Correct	Incorrect	Correct
timerity	temerity	toam	tome
timerus	timorous	tobacca	tobacco
timmathy	timothy	toboggen	toboggan
timmid	timid	tocatta	toccata
timpanni	timpani	tocco	taco
timpestuous	tempestuous	tocsen	tocsin (alarm)
timplate	template	tocsen	toxin (poison)
timpo	tempo	toddey	toddy
timporal	temporal	tode	toad
tinchure	tincture	toehee	towhee
tiney	tiny	toel	toil
tingel	tingle	toffey	toffee
tinje	tinge	toffu	tofu
tinkel	tinkle	togather	together
tinnitis	tinnitus	togga	toga
tinsle	tinsel	toggel	toggle
tinsor	tensor	toillet	toilet
tintinabullation	tintinnabulation	Toj Moholl	Taj Mahal
tippel	tipple	tokin	token
tippit	tippet	Tokio	Tokyo
tipsey	tipsy	tole road	toll road
tirrade	tirade	tollerable	tolerable
tishew	tissue	tollerance	tolerance
titannic	titanic	tollerate	tolerate
tite	tight	tomfoolary	tomfoolery
titen	tighten	tommahawk	tomahawk
tith	tithe	tommato	tomato
tittalate	titillate	tommography	tomography
tittilating	titillating	tommorrow	tomorrow
tittmouse	titmouse	tondra	tundra
tittular	titular	tongue oil	tung oil
tmessis	tmesis	tonnight	tonight
toadey	toady	tonnometer	tonometer
toak	toque (hat)	tonnow	tonneau

Incorrect	Correct	Incorrect	Correct
tonsallectomy	tonsillectomy	torrment	torment
tonsillitus	tonsillitis	torrso	torso
tonsills	tonsils	torrte	torte
tonsoreal	tonsorial	torrus	torus
tonsurre	tonsure	torsien	torsion
tont	taunt	tortacollis	torticollis
tonteen	tontine	tortonni	tortoni
toocan	toucan	tortous	tortuous
toomstone	tombstone	tortuss	tortoise
toomult	tumult	Toscannini	Toscanini
toomultuous	tumultuous	tostadda	tostada
toopay	toupee	totalitarean	totalitarian
too-too	tutu	totall	total
tooty-frooty	tutti-frutti	totallaty	totality
topiery	topiary	totum	totem
toppaz	topaz	touchay	touché
toppee	topee	touff	tough
toppic	topic	tournamment	tournament
toppography	topography	tourniquit	tourniquet
toppology	topology	tourrism	tourism
topsee-turvey	topsy-turvy	tourrist	tourist
torchure	torture	toushay	touché
torerro	torero	toxicollogy	toxicology
tork	torque	toxxic	toxic
Torkeymada	Torquemada	toxxin	toxin
tornaido	tornado	traccion	traction
torped	torpid	trachiotomy	tracheotomy
torpeedo	torpedo	trackea	trachea
torper	torpor	trackt	tract
Torra	Torah	tractabel	tractable
torreador	toreador	tracter	tractor
torred	torrid	traddition	tradition
torrensial	torrential	tradditionel	traditional
torrant	torrent	tradduce	traduce

Incorrect	Correct	Incorrect	Correct
traggedy	tragedy	translitterate	transliterate
traggicomedy	tragicomedy	translusent	translucent
traiterous	traitorous	transmision	transmission
trajectary	trajectory	transmittel	transmittal
trammil	trammel	transmittible	transmittable
trampalline	trampoline	transmoggrafy	transmogrify
trancient	transient	transmutacion	transmutation
tranquillizer	tranqualizer	transparation	transpiration
tranquallity	tranquility, or tranquillity	transparrency	transparency
		transparrent	transparent
tranquill	tranquil	transpier	transpire
transaccion	transaction	transpoes	transpose
transative	transitive	transubstansiate	transubstantiate
transcendant	transcendent	transum	transom
transcendentel	transcendental	Transval	Transvaal
transciever	transceiver	transversel	transversal
transcrip	transcript	transvestitte	transvestite
transcripsion	transcription	trapeez	trapeze
transdusser	transducer	trapezeum	trapezium
transe	trance	trapezeus	trapezius
transend	transcend	trappazoid	trapezoid
transet	transit	trapse	traipse
transexuel	transsexual	trataria	trattoria
transfered	transferred	trator	traitor
transferrence	transference	traul	trawl
transfigurration	transfiguration	trauler	trawler
transformasion	transformation	traumma	trauma
transfussion	transfusion	traummatize	traumatize
transgres	transgress	travale	travail
transgresion	transgression	travellogue	travelogue
transister	transistor	travveled	traveled
transitorry	transitory	travveler	traveler
translacion	translation	travverse	traverse

Incorrect	Correct	Incorrect	Correct
travvesty	travesty	trianguler	triangular
treackly	treacly	triangullar	triangular
treadel	treadle	Triasic	Triassic
treage	triage	triathalon	triathlon
treasson	treason	triballism	tribalism
treasurey	treasury	tribbulations	tribulations
treay	tray (for food)	Tribecka	TriBeCa
treay	trey (three)	tribul	tribal
treazure	treasure	tribunnal	tribunal
trebble	treble	tributerry	tributary
trecharry	treachery	tricenteneal	tricentennial
trecherous	treacherous	trickel	trickle
trecked	trekked	trickinosis	trichinosis
tred	tread	tricusspid	tricuspid
treecle	treacle	tridant	trident
treeson	treason	trieneal	triennial
treetice	treatise	trifeckta	trifecta
trefoile	trefoil	trifel	trifle
treking	trekking	trifoccals	trifocals
trekk	trek	trifthong	triphthong
trellise	trellis	trigemminal	trigeminal
tremallo	tremolo	triggonometry	trigonometry
tremmatode	trematode	triglisseride	triglyceride
tremmendous	tremendous	trilatteral	trilateral
tremmor	tremor	trilinguel	trilingual
tremmulous	tremulous	trilleon	trillion
trenchent	trenchant	trilleum	trillium
treppidation	trepidation	trillobite	trilobite
tres	tress	trillogy	trilogy
tressle	trestle	trimarran	trimaran
tresspass	trespass	trimble	tremble
tressure	treasure	trimmester	trimester
triangel	triangle	trimmeter	trimeter

Incorrect	Correct	Incorrect	Correct
trinch	trench	troope	troop (soldier)
trind	trend	troope	troupe (group)
trinkit	trinket	trophey	trophy
trinnity	trinity	troppe	trope
tripartitte	tripartite	troppic	tropic
triphibbian	triphibian	troppical	tropical
trippe	tripe	troppopause	tropopause
tripple sec	triple sec	troubaddor	troubadour
tripplets	triplets	trouf	trough
triptic	triptych	trounse	trounce
trise	trice	trouppe	troop (soldier)
triseratops	triceratops	trouppe	troupe (group)
triskadekkaphobia		troupps	troops
	triskaidekaphobia	trouzers	trousers
triskellion	triskelion	trowell	trowel
trissect	trisect	trratzo	terrazzo
trist	tryst	trubble	trouble
tritheeism	tritheism	trucculent	truculent
trittium	tritium	truely	truly
triumfant	triumphant	truency	truancy
triumff	triumph	truent	truant
triumvirr	triumvir	truesso	trousseau
triumvirrate	triumvirate	truffel	truffle
trivvet	trivet	trumpit	trumpet
trivvia	trivia	trunchon	truncheon
trivvial	trivial	trunkate	truncate
troff	trough	trus	truss
trogladite	troglodyte	trustey	trustee
trokaic	trochaic	truthfull	truthful
trokee	trochee	tryad	triad
trolle	troll	trybunals	tribunals
trolly	trolley	trygliceride	triglyceride
tromboan	trombone	tryreme	trireme
tromp le oil	trompe l'oeil	tsarr	tsar

Incorrect	Correct	Incorrect	Correct
tseat-see fly	tsetse fly	turnbuckel	turnbuckle
tsumani	tsunami	turnstyle	turnstile
tubba	tuba	turnup	turnip
tubberculosis	tuberculosis	turpatude	turpitude
tubercule	tubercle	turpintine	turpentine
tubercullar	tubercular	Turpshickory	Terpsichore
tubullar	tubular	turquoese	turquoise
tuch	touch	turreen	tureen
Tuddor	Tudor	turrit	turret
tuission	tuition	turse	terse
tulep	tulip	Tuscanny	Tuscany
tumbel	tumble	tussell	tussle
tumbelweed	tumbleweed	tutilary	tutelary
tumbrell	tumbrel	tutellage	tutelage
tumesence	tumescence	Tutonnic	Teutonic
tumesent	tumescent	tutoreal	tutorial
tumesis	tmesis	tuttor	tutor
tunell	tunnel	tuxido	tuxedo
tungstin	tungsten	twaing	twang
tungue	tongue	twane	twain
tunick	tunic	twealfth	twelfth
tupello	tupelo	tweazers	tweezers
turbajet	turbojet	tweek	tweak
turbed	turbid	twell	twill
turbin	turban (headwear)	twenge	twinge
		twentyeth	twentieth
turbinne	turbine (rotor)	twien	twine
turbulant	turbulent	twigg	twig
turbullence	turbulence	twille	twill
turbut	turbot	twillight	twilight
ture	tour	twinkel	twinkle
turjid	turgid	twofur	twofer
turmoile	turmoil	tyfoon	typhoon
turmuric	turmeric	tympanni	tympani

Incorrect	Correct	Incorrect	Correct
tympannic	tympanic	**typpicly**	typically
tympannim	tympanum	**tyrannicle**	tyrannical
typhess	typhus	**tyrannisaur**	tyrannosaur
typhoyd	typhoid	**tyrenny**	tyranny
typographicle	typographical	**tyrent**	tyrant
typollogy	typology	**tyrranize**	tyrannize

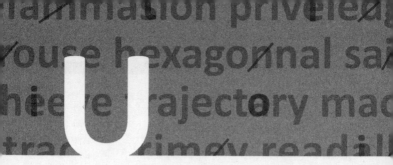

Most Commonly Misspelled Words

- ultimately
- umbrella
- uncomfortable
- unconscious
- underneath
- unfriendly
- until
- unwieldy
- useful
- usually

Incorrect	Correct	Incorrect	Correct
ubbiquitous	ubiquitous	unbenone	unbeknown
ucase	ukase	uncanney	uncanny
uddar	udder	uncion	unction
ugennics	eugenics	uncomfortible	uncomfortable
uggsome	ugsome	uncommited	uncommitted
uglefy	uglify	uncommunacative	uncommunicative
ugly fruit	ugli fruit	unconcionable	unconscionable
ukalali	ukulele	unconditionnal	unconditional
Ukrain	Ukraine	unconsious	unconscious
ulagee	eulogy	unconstatutional	unconstitutional
ullna	ulna	uncooth	uncouth
ullser	ulcer	unctous	unctuous
ullterior	ulterior	undalent fever	undulant fever
ulltimatly	ultimately	undawnted	undaunted
ultamatim	ultimatum	undenyable	undeniable
ultimitt	ultimate	undereport	underreport
ultramountain	ultramontane	underestimmate	underestimate
ultraviollet	ultraviolet	undergradduate	undergraduate
ulullate	ululate	underminne	undermine
Ulysees	Ulysses	undernurrish	undernourish
umbillacal	umbilical	underprivilleged	underprivileged
umbillicus	umbilicus	underun	underrun
umble	umbel	underwhilm	underwhelm
umbow	umbo	undessirable	undesirable
umbrige	umbrage	undocummented	undocumented
umeack	umiak	undullating	undulating
umlout	umlaut	uneeque	unique
ummbra	umbra	unemploymant	unemployment
ummbrella	umbrella	unequivoccal	unequivocal
unacelluler	unicellular	unfamilliar	unfamiliar
unannamous	unanimous	unfavvorable	unfavorable
unavoidible	unavoidable	unflappible	unflappable
unballanced	unbalanced	unflenching	unflinching
unbelievible	unbelievable	unforgettible	unforgettable

Incorrect	Correct	Incorrect	Correct
unfrendly	unfriendly	unnique	unique
unganly	ungainly	unnison	unison
ungraceous	ungracious	unnity	unity
ungullate	ungulate	unparralleled	unparalleled
ungwent	unguent	unpoppular	unpopular
unhalloed	unhallowed	unprejudised	unprejudiced
unhenge	unhinge	unpremedditated	unpremeditated
unicammeral	unicameral	unpressadented	unprecedented
unick	eunuch	unprofessionnal	unprofessional
uniformitty	uniformity	unquallified	unqualified
unilateral	unilateral	unreadible	unreadable
unimpeachible	unimpeachable	unreallistic	unrealistic
unintellagible	unintelligible	unreasonnable	unreasonable
unipollar	unipolar	unrellenting	unrelenting
Unitarean	Unitarian	unremmiting	unremitting
universel	universal	unrivvaled	unrivaled or unrivalled
universitty	university		
unkimpt	unkempt	unsaturrated	unsaturated
unknowible	unknowable	unscruppalous	unscrupulous
unlawfull	unlawful	unseasonnable	unseasonable
unleesh	unleash	unsial	uncial
unlimmited	unlimited	unsociabel	unsociable
unmentionible	unmentionable	unsofisticated	unsophisticated
unmercifull	unmerciful	unspeakible	unspeakable
unmisteakable	unmistakable	unstenting	unstinting
unmittigated	unmitigated	unstructurred	unstructured
unnabridged	unabridged	untennable	untenable
unnambiguously	unambiguously	untill	until
unnasalable	unassailable	untouchible	untouchable
unnaturel	unnatural	untutorred	untutored
unndderneath	underneath	unutterrable	unutterable
unnecesary	unnecessary	unvailing	unveiling
unnicorn	unicorn	unweildy	unwieldy
unnicycle	unicycle	Upannishads	Upanishads

Incorrect	Correct	Incorrect	Correct
upbrade	upbraid	Urssa Major	Ursa Major
upheavel	upheaval	urstwhile	erstwhile
upholsterry	upholstery	usafruct	usufruct
uppitty	uppity	usefull	useful
uprorrious	uproarious	ushar	usher
upsillon	upsilon	usible	usable
upsy dazy	upsy daisy	uskabaw	usquebaugh
Uraguay	Uruguay	usorreous	usurious
urannium	uranium	usorrious	usurious
urbain	urbane	ussurp	usurp
urbanisation	urbanization	ussurpacion	usurpation
urbannaty	urbanity	ussury	usury
urben	urban	usuelly	usually
urbenize	urbanize	usufruc	usufruct
urchen	urchin	usurrer	usurer
ureeter	ureter	utensel	utensil
ureethra	urethra	uterrine	uterine
uremea	uremia	uterrus	uterus
urethain	urethane	uthenasia	euthanasia
urethrascope	urethroscope	utilitarrian	utilitarian
urgensey	urgency	utillity	utility
urgg	erg	utopea	utopia
urgott	ergot	utopean	utopian
urinnal	urinal	uttar	utter
urinnate	urinate	utterence	utterance
urremia	uremia	uvia	uvea
urrine	urine	uvulu	uvula
urrn	urn	uxorreal	uxorial
urrology	urology	uxorreous	uxorious
ursotz	ersatz		

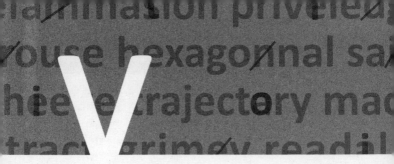

Most Commonly Misspelled Words

- vacuum
- valuable
- vanilla
- variation
- vegetable
- version
- village
- vibrant
- villain
- violet

Incorrect	Correct	Incorrect	Correct
vaccancy	vacancy	vandel	vandal
vaccate	vacate	vandellism	vandalism
vaccation	vacation	vannella	vanilla
vaccsine	vaccine	vannish	vanish
vaccum	vacuum	vannity	vanity
vaccuous	vacuous	vanquesh	vanquish
vacinity	vicinity	vaont	vaunt
vackuity	vacuity	vaoult	vault
vacsination	vaccination	vaparize	vaporize
vadde meecum	vade mecum	vaper	vapor
vaggabond	vagabond	vappid	vapid
vaggary	vagary	vaquerro	vaquero
vaggina	vagina	varicose	varicose
vagransy	vagrancy	varment	varmint
vail	vale (valley)	varnesh	varnish
vail	veil (cloth worn over the face)	varriable	variable
		varriance	variance
valdictorean	valedictorian	varriant	variant
valerean	valerian	varriatel	varietal
vallatudinarian	valetudinarian	varriation	variation
vallay	valet	varricose	varicose
vallence	valance	varrience	variance
valliant	valiant	varriety	variety
vallidate	validate	varriform	variform
vallidity	validity	varrigated	variegated
vallise	valise	varriorum	variorum
vallor	valor	varrious	various
vallorous	valorous	varsatee	varsity
valuble	valuable	vasculur	vascular
valuntine	valentine	vasillate	vacillate
vammoose	vamoose	vassectomy	vasectomy
vampyre	vampire	vassel	vassal
Van gohe	Van Gogh	Vasseline	Vaseline
vandallize	vandalize	Vasser	Vassar

Incorrect	Correct	Incorrect	Correct
vassilation	vacillation	vellure	velour
vassodilator	vasodilator	Veltenshong	Weltanschauung
Vattican	Vatican	velvateen	velveteen
vau	vow	velvetty	velvety
vaudville	vaudeville	velvit	velvet
vauge	vague	vem	vim
vauntid	vaunted	Ven diagram	Venn diagram
vayne	vain (futile, overly proud)	venallaty	venality
		venchure	venture
vayne	vane (fan blade)	vendeta	vendetta
vea medea	via media	vendictive	vindictive
vear	veer	vengiance	vengeance
veche	vetch	venil	venal
vecter	vector	Venise	Venice
veegan	vegan	vennder	vendor
veel	veal	Vennecian	Venetian
veenial	venial	venneer	veneer
veggitarian	vegetarian	vennel	venal
veggitate	vegetate	vennerable	venerable
vegitible	vegetable	vennerate	venerate
vehemment	vehement	vennereal	venereal
vehiccle	vehicle	vennison	venison
vehicullar	vehicular	vennue	venue
veild	veldt, or veld	ventalate	ventilate
Veit Nam	Vietnam	ventalation	ventilation
veiwpoint	viewpoint	ventrel	ventral
vell	vale (valley)	ventrilloquism	ventriloquism
vell	veil (cloth worn over the face)	venu	venue
		verago	virago
vellam	vellum (paper)	verasimilatude	verisimilitude
vellam	velum (mouth part)	verasity	veracity
		verballize	verbalize
Vellcro	Velcro	verbatem	verbatim
vellossapede	velocipede	verbege	verbiage

Incorrect	Correct	Incorrect	Correct
verbel	verbal	vertiggo	vertigo
verboce	verbose	vertiginnous	vertiginous
verdent	verdant	vertual	virtual
verdeur	verdure	vertue	virtue
veridicle	veridical	vertuosity	virtuosity
verile	virile	vertuoso	virtuoso
verilunt	virulent	verzion	version
verizmo	verismo	vespars	vespers
verje	verge	vespir	vesper
verman	vermin	vessal	vessel
vermay	vermeil	vessical	vesicle
vermicceli	vermicelli	Vessuvious	Vesuvius
vermicullate	vermiculate (worm-eaten)	vestabule	vestibule
		vestel virgin	vestal virgin
vermicullite	vermiculite (mineral)	vestigeal	vestigial
		vestij	vestige
vermillion	vermilion	veteren	veteran
vernacullar	vernacular	vetterinarian	veterinarian
vernel	vernal	vexacious	vexatious
vernisage	vernissage	viabble	viable
veronnica	veronica	viabillity	viability
verracious	veracious	vialet	violet
verracity	veracity	vibbration	vibration
verranda	veranda	vibirnum	viburnum
verrify	verify	vibratto	vibrato
verrioram	variorum	vibrent	vibrant
verrity	verity	vicarrious	vicarious
Versales	Versailles	viccar	vicar
versatille	versatile	vicinnity	vicinity
versefication	versification	vicissatude	vicissitude
versis	versus	vicount	viscount
vertabra	vertebra	vicunna	vicuna
vertabrate	vertebrate	videllacit	videlicet
verticle	vertical	vidiographer	videographer

Incorrect	Correct	Incorrect	Correct
vieing	vying	violasion	violation
vien	vein (ore, blood)	violinnist	violinist
viggel	vigil	violla	viola
vigger	vigor	violla de gamba	viola da gamba
viggerous	vigorous	viollate	violate
vigillance	vigilance	viollated	violated
vigillanty	vigilante (person)	viollence	violence
vigillent	vigilant (watchful)	viollent	violent
Vikking	Viking	viollin	violin
villafication	vilification	viraggo	virago
villafy	vilify	viras	virus
villege	village	virdict	verdict
villian	villain	virgen	virgin
villinelle	villanelle	virginel	virginal
vinal	vinyl	virginnity	virginity
vindacate	vindicate	virgulle	virgule
vindalou	vindaloo	virille	virile
vingeance	vengeance	virracity	veracity
vinnager	vinegar	virralent	virulent
vinnagrette	vinaigrette	virranda	veranda
Vinnecian	Venetian	virsatile	versatile
vinnette	vignette	virtex	vertex
vinnison	venison	virtuely	virtually
vintige	vintage	virtuil	virtual
vintillate	ventilate	virtuositty	virtuosity
vintnurr	vintner	vis-a-vee	vis-a-vis
vintrillaquism	ventriloquism	viscious	vicious (mean)
vinture	venture	viscossity	viscosity
vinu	venue	viscus	viscose (fabric), viscous (sticky)
vinyard	vineyard		
vinyet	vignette	viser	visor
violla	viola (stringed instrument	viseroy	viceroy
		Vishnoo	Vishnu
viola de amor	viola d'amore	vishysoisse	vichyssoise

Incorrect	Correct	Incorrect	Correct
visibillity	visibility	vollatillaty	volatility
visionery	visionary	vollition	volition
vissage	visage	volltage	voltage
Vissagoth	Visigoth	volluble	voluble
visserel	visceral	vollume	volume
vissiate	vitiate	volluptuous	voluptuous
vission	vision	volly	volley
vissit	visit	vol-o-vent	vol-au-vent
vissitation	visitation	Volpoorgis night	Walpurgis night
vissitor	visitor	Voltair	Voltaire
vissta	vista	volumminous	voluminous
vitallity	vitality	voluntery	voluntary
vitel	vital	voluptuery	voluptuary
vitreol	vitriol	vommit	vomit
vitrius	vitreous	vorracious	voracious
vittals	vittles	vortecs	vortex
vittamin	vitamin	vouche	vouch
vittreolic	vitriolic	voug	vogue
vituprative	vituperative	vowwel	vowel
vivvacity	vivacity	vox poppuli	vox populi
vivvid	vivid	voyd	void
vixxen	vixen	voyure	voyeur
vizual	visual	vulcannize	vulcanize
vocabulery	vocabulary	vulchoor	vulture
vocal chords	vocal cords	vulgarrity	vulgarity
vocallize	vocalize	vullva	vulva
vocifferous	vociferous	vulnerbal	vulnerable
vodoo	voodoo	vwale	voile
Vognerian	Wagnerian	vyaduct	viaduct
volatil	volatile	vyal	vial
volcannic	volcanic	vye	vie
volcanno	volcano	Vymar	Weimar
voll	vole		

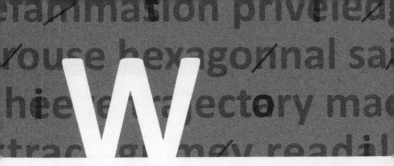

Most Commonly Misspelled Words

- wagon
- warfare
- warrant
- waste
- weather
- weird
- wheelbarrow
- whether
- willful
- writing

Incorrect	Correct	Incorrect	Correct
waddel	waddle	warior	warrior
waddy	wadi	warmunger	warmonger
wafe	waif	warrent	warrant
waffel	waffle	warrenty	warranty
waffer	wafer	waspesh	waspish
waggon	wagon	wassabi	wasabi
wain	wane	wassale	wassail
wainright	wainwright	wasteril	wastrel
waistrel	wastrel	watchfull	watchful
waitt	wait	water lilly	water lily
wajer	wager	waterbourn	waterborne
wakefull	wakeful	watermellon	watermelon
Wakiki	Waikiki	wattnot	whatnot
wallabee	wallaby	waeve	wave (hand gesture), waive (relinquish)
Walldorf	Waldorf		
wallett	wallet		
wallnut	walnut	wavey	wavy
wallo	wallow	wavver	waiver (legal form)
Wallpurgis Night	Walpurgis Night		
		wavver	waver (to go back and forth)
wallup	wallop		
walruss	walrus	waxxen	waxen
wampam	wampum	wayfairer	wayfarer
wandar	wander	wayle	wail
Wankle engine	Wankel engine	waynscot	wainscot
wann	wan	wayst	waist
warbaler	warbler	wayste	waste
warbel	warble	wearysome	wearisome
wardin	warden	weathar	weather
warenty	warranty	weathir	weather (meteorological conditions)
warey	wary		
warf	wharf		
warfair	warfare	weathir	whether (if)
warilly	warily	Wedgewoud	Wedgwood

Incorrect	Correct	Incorrect	Correct
ween	wean	whesk	whisk
weerd	weird	whiley	wily
weery	weary	whinnie	whinny
weevel	weevil	whipoorwill	whippoorwill
weezel	weasel	whirlygig	whirligig
wegeela	weigela	whiskee	whiskey
weighword	wayward	whodunnet	whodunit
Weimaroner	Weimaraner	whoe	whoa
weinch	wench	wholistic	holistic
weiner	wiener	whollsome	wholesome
Weinner shnitzel	Wiener schnitzel	whorf	wharf
wellfare	welfare	wiave	waive
wellterweight	welterweight	wiaver	waiver
welp	whelp	Wickon	Wiccan
Weltenshong	Weltanschauung	widgitt	widget
welthy	wealthy	wiegh	weigh
Wendsday	Wednesday	wieght	weight
werwolf	werewolf	wier	weir
wesk	whisk	wierd	weird
Westminnister	Westminster	wildabeast	wildebeest
wheadle	wheedle	willfull	willful
wheal	wheel	winn	wen (tumor)
whealp	whelp	winn	win (victory)
wheather	weather (meteorologic conditions)	winable	winnable
		Windser knot	Windsor knot
		winsum	winsome
wheather	whether (if)	wipper	wiper
wheelborrow	wheelbarrow	wirey	wiry
whelke	whelk	wirst	worst (most bad)
whem	whim	wirst	wurst (sausage)
whemsical	whimsical	wirsted	worsted (cloth)
whense	whence	wishey-washee	wishy-washy
wherewithall	wherewithal	wishfull	wishful
wherrabouts	whereabouts	wissenhimer	wisenheimer

Incorrect	Correct	Incorrect	Correct
wist	whist	wormth	warmth
wistiria	wisteria	worrysome	worrisome
wistle	whistle	wrastle	wrestle
withold	withhold	wraught	wrought
witnisses	witnesses	wrech	retch (gag)
wittacism	witticism	wrech	wretch (person)
wizzard	wizard	wreck havvock	wreak havoc
wobegone	woebegone	wreckege	wreckage
woddi	wadi	wreckless	reckless
wode	woad	wreek	wreak
woft	waft	wreeth	wreath (noun)
wollop	wallop	wreeth	wreathe (verb)
wolverrine	wolverine	wreng	wring
wonderfull	wonderful	wrenkle	wrinkle
wonderlust	wanderlust	wrey	wry
wontahn	wonton (Chinese dumpling)	wreyneck	wryneck
		wriethe	writhe
wonten	wanton (reckless)	wrighte	wright (suffix) write (letters)
wooley	woolly	wrinch	wrench
woond	wound	writting	writing
Woostershire	Worcestershire	wunt	wont (accustomed), won't (will not)
wopiti	wapiti		
worforen	warfarin		
worlock	warlock	wyvvern	wyvern

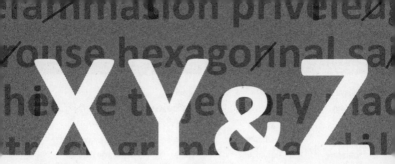

X Y & Z

Most Commonly Misspelled Words

- xylophone
- yacht
- yesterday
- yield
- yogurt
- you're
- your
- zeal
- zephyr
- zoology

Incorrect	Correct	Incorrect	Correct
xinnya	zinnia	yooel	yule
Yahway	Yahweh	Yosimmatee	Yosemite
yakk	yak	yott	yacht
yammar	yammer	youre	your (you own)
yarlsberg	Jarlsberg	youre	you're (contraction of "you are")
yarmulka	yarmulke		
yarr	yare		
yarro	yarrow	yucka	yucca
yaul	yawl	yufoneum	euphonium
yaun	yawn	yufonius	euphonious
y-chromasome	y-chromosome	yuforea	euphoria
yeest	yeast	yuforric	euphoric
yeild	yield	Yum Kippur	Yom Kippur
yenn	yen	yupey	yuppie
yenn and yang	yin and yang	Yurapean	European
yert	yurt	Yurasian	Eurasian
yesheva	yeshiva	yureeka	eureka
yesterrday	yesterday	yurn	yearn
yetty	yeti	yuro	euro
yewe	ewe	yuthanasia	euthanasia
yewer	ewer	yuthfull	youthful
yinn	yin	zaar	tzar
yinta	yenta	zaney	zany
yipee	yippee	Zanthippy	Xanthippe
yoak	yoke (collar)	zeebra	zebra
yodaling	yodeling	zeel	zeal
yoddel	yodel	zeelot	zealot
yoeman	yeoman	zeenith	zenith
yogart	yogurt	zennia	zinnia
yogee	yogi (person)	zenophobiz	xenophobia
yogga	yoga (practice)	zeppalin	zeppelin
yokle	yokel	zeppher	zephyr
yolke	yolk (egg)	zerros	zeroes
yoo	yew	Zerrox	Xerox

Incorrect	Correct	Incorrect	Correct
Zietgiest	Zeitgeist	zoollagy	zoology
ziffoid	xiphoid	Zoony	Zuni
ziggerat	ziggurat	Zorastrean	Zoroastrian
zinck	zinc	zoro	Zorro
Zinfendel	Zinfandel	zweeback	zwieback
zinnon	xenon	zydecco	zydeco
zirkon	zircon	zygoat	zygote
zithar	zither	zylaphone	xylophone
zodiak	zodiac	zylom	xylem
zofftig	zaftig	zymergy	zymurgy
zoogma	zeugma		

Appendix: Spell It Right Now

CAUTION

If only everything had a rule you could count on! The following rules are helpful—but, like most things in life, only up to a point. Since nothing is perfect, *do* use the aid these provide, but also be aware that an exception may pop up at any moment.

- An **abbé** is a member of the clergy. **Abby** (or **Abbey** or **Abbie**) is a woman's name. An **abbey** is a monastery or a church.

- Like any term transliterated from a different alphabet, **al Qaeda** is spelled in different ways. But you're likely to be safe with this widely accepted form of the Arabic term for "the base."

- A woman graduate is an **alumna**. Women are **alumnae**. A man is an **alumnus**. Men are **alumni**. Graduates in a mixed-gender group are also called **alumni**.

- An **auger** is a device with spiral threads—like a drill-bit. To **augur** is to predict, especially through signs or omens.

- **Bass**, when pronounced with a long "a" (sounds like **base**) means "low," as in "bass horn." When it has a short "a" sound (rhymes with "lass"), it refers to a fish.

- A **bole** is a tree-trunk; a **boll** is a round seed-container of plants such as cotton or flax; a **bowl** is a wide, deep dish; to **bowl** is to roll a ball at tenpins.

- In India, **brahman** is a title of respect; it's also the name for a breed of cattle. A **Brahmin** is a member of a cultural or social elite, as in a ***Boston Brahmin***. (Note: **Brahmin** is considered a variant of **Brahman** for both people and cattle, although both spellings are in fairly common use.)

- **Calvary** is the name of a hill; **cavalry** refers to troops on horseback.

- A **censer** is a dish for burning incense. A **sensor** detects the presence of something. A **censor** is someone who tries to remove or suppress something considered objectionable. To **censure** (sin-sure) is to criticize harshly.

- The **core** is the center of something; a **corps** is a group of people (often a military group, like the Marine Corps), a **corpse** is no longer alive.

- To **dissemble** is to conceal the truth, to act or speak hypocritically. To **disassemble** is to take apart.

- Watch out for **its** and **it's**. If you'll think of the apostrophe in **it's** as a little floating "i," this will help you remember that **it's** means **it is** (or sometimes **it has**). And **its** is a possessive pronoun, so you could say "**It's** time for the dog to have **its** dinner."

- **Kudos**, meaning "praise," may look like a plural, but it isn't. So there is no **kudo**.

- **Liable** (three syllables) is a formal term for "legally responsible," and informal for "likely to." **Libel** (two syllables) refers to the crime of defaming someone in writing. "You're **liable** to be **liable** for **libel**."

- **Liqueur** [lick ERR] is the sweet, strongly flavored alcoholic beverage drunk after dinner. **Liquor** [LICK er] is the more generic distilled alcoholic beverage, such as whiskey or gin.

- Be careful with the tricky French ending of **longueur**. You'll also find it in **liqueur**.

- Watch out for the strange combinations of letters in both halves of the word **maelstrom**. From the Dutch for "whirling stream," this word has nothing to do with **male** or **storm**.

- In **occurrence**, the "r" doubles to help establish that the vowel sound in **occur** doesn't change. Similarly: **occurring**.

- Both **renaissance** (REN a sance) and **renascence** (ren ASS ance) are acceptable forms of the word meaning "rebirth." In the United States you'll more often see and hear the first form.

- To **review** something is to go over it again. A **review** is a written evaluation, often of a book, play, or other work of art. A **revue** is a variety show of skits, songs, and other material, often satirical.

- **Saccharin** is a sugar substitute. But **saccharine** is the spelling for the adjective describing people—or books or movies—that are somewhat sickly sweet.

- A **secret** is something you keep private, but **secrete** (suh KREET) is a verb that can mean to hide something away or, in reference to the body, to generate a substance.

- You'll often see **sulphur** as well as **sulfer**, particularly in older writing. But don't confuse either with **sulfa** drugs.

- **Sine** is a mathematical function, not to be confused with the common word **sign** or the word in the Scots dialect phrase auld lang **syne**.

- You'll also see **travelled** for the past tense of travel, but **traveled** is more frequent in the United States.

- Don't confuse **write**, the common verb for forming words on paper, with **right** (the opposite of wrong) or **rite** (a ceremony or ritual)—not to mention **wright**, a suffix for a maker of something.

MEMORY HOOKS

You'll also hear memory hooks called by their more formal term "mnemonic devices." It comes from Mnemosyne, the Greek goddess of memory. Before you go on to our samples, understand that the idea is to learn to make up your own mnemonics. Some of the sentences you make up will be pretty silly—and that's fine. You're not trying to write great literature; you're trying to make up a sentence that will help you spell troublesome words!

- To remember the difference between **adopt** and **adapt**, use the middle letter of each word. The "a" reminds us that to **adapt** something is to change it, and to **adopt** it is to take it as your **o**wn.

- **Adverse** usually refers to things or conditions, while **averse** refers to people: "She was **averse** to moving to Iceland because of the **adverse** weather conditions there." Notice that the one with the "d" refers to **d**umb (unthinking) things—not people.

- **Appraise** means "evaluate," and **apprise** means "inform." When you meet with your supervisor for your performance **appraisal**, you'd like to get **praise**, and maybe even a **raise**. And the word with a simple "i" means to **i**nform. So you'd say "Please **appraise** the situation, and keep me **apprised**."

- Most **capitOl** buildings have a dOme on top. **Capital** means "important, major, serious"—capital city, capital idea, capital letter, capital punishment.

- **Complement** means **to complete** or **something that completes**. To **compliment** is to say something **nice**. So link the "i" in nice to compliment, or the "e" in complete to complement.

- A **council** is a group of people who meet for a common purpose. **Counsel** can mean to **advise** someone, and either the advisor or the advice itself can be called **counsel**. Link **council** (the one with the internal "c" not "s") to **committee** (which begins with a "c").

- To remember that **eminent** refers to **people** who are outstanding in their professions, think "h**E** and sh**E** are **Eminent**." And to remember that **imminent** refers to a thing or event that is very likely to happen soon, think "**It** is **Imminent**."

- If you'll mentally link the **E** at the beginning of **Emigrate** to **Exit**, it will help you remember that to **emigrate** is to move **out of** a country or place. And linking the first letter of **Immigrate** to **Into** will remind you that **Immigrants** are people who move **Into** a country or place.

- Roman numerals can help you remember how to spell **existence**. Just trim an **e** off each end, then think "X is ten, C (see)?"

- A **floe** is a flat expanse of floating ice. To remember that **flow** refers to moving current, link the last letter in **floW** to the first letter in **Water**. (And you could link the last letter in **floE** to the first letter in **Expanse**.)

- **Forego** means "to go before" (hint: link **fore** and **before**). To **forgo** means "to go without" (and it's the one that **goes without the e**). Example: The **foregoing** hint will help you remember how to spell these words, but that doesn't mean you can **forgo** using this handy book.

- **Hangar** (with an "a") names the building where **A**irplanes are kept. A **hanger** (with an "e") may be used for hanging clothes and just about **E**verything **E**lse.

- **Ingenuous** (in-JEN-you-us) means "innocent, naïve, perhaps easily fooled." But **ingenious** (in-GENIUS) means "clever, bright, inventive"—and this one has a built-in memory hook, because the last part sounds like **genius**.

- Remember the **leopard's** big-cat cousin, **Leo** the Lion.

- The **mambo** is a lively dance. The **mamba** is a snake whose bite is often fatal. To remember which is which, you can mentally link the "a" at the end of mamba to the "a" in both snake and fatal.

- Because of the plague, it was easy to **die** in the me**die**val period.

- It is ne**cess**ary to have a **cess**pool.

- **Oleo** (short for oleomargarine) is a butter-substitute spread. An **olio** is a stew with many different ingredients—or any mixture of different things. Hint—link the **i** in **olio** to the **i** in m**i**x.

- Think "**I am** a member of parl**iam**ent" to get those middle vowels right.

- The European Union (EU) requires milk to be past**eu**rized.

- The phar**ao**h gets mail at **AO**L.

- To help keep that easily-forgettable second e in **plebeian**, remember that West Point calls a first-year student a **plebe**.

- A **quarry** can be something hunted or a pit where stone is mined. A **query** is a question, and that gives you a good memory hook—the "que-" at the beginning of **que**stion and **que**ry.

- Although **quay** is pronounced "key," it has its own "qurazy" spelling.

- Remember the "c" that leads off the last syllable of **regicide** with this understated thought: "if you kill a king, you deprive him of his **c**rown."

- Etch this memorably silly sentence in your head: "**R**ide **H**ard, **Y**ou **T**hick-**H**eaded **M**onster." That's how you spell **rhythm**.

- One of the most common exceptions to the old "i before e rule" is **seize**. "Do NOT seize the sieve in a siege" is our corny mnemonic to remember how this word differs from the other two.

- **Silhouette** comes from the name of a Frenchman. Keep the "h" in the word by remembering "he" lives on in this word.

- The unusual "-sede" ending **supersedes** all other spellings. This is said to be the only word in the English languge ending in "sede."

- The verb **teethe**, which rhymes with **seethe**, refers to a baby's acquiring teeth. "Baby Joe is irritable because he is **teething**."

- Help yourself get the spelling of **their** right by thinking of the phrase "**their heir**looms." And don't confuse this possessive pronoun with **there**, the opposite of **here**.

TRICKY TWINS AND TRIPLETS

Watch out for non-identical twins and first cousins in the world of language. Some of these words are homonyms (pronounced alike but spelled differently), and some are close in spelling and thus easily confused.

- An **afterword** is a short piece of writing added at the end of a book—some **words after** the main part. **Afterward** means "at a later time."

- An **altar** is a stand or table in a place of worship. **Alter** means "other" (as in alter ego, alternate, etc.), and as a verb to **alter** means "to change."

- An **arc** is a curve, a part of a circle. An **ark** is a boat, or an enclosure in a temple.

- An **axle** is a shaft that wheels are mounted on. An **Axel** is a figure-skater's leap, named for its inventor, Axel Paulson. An **axil** is an angle between parts of a plant (e.g., between leaf and stem).

- A **ballad** is a popular song, often sentimental. A **ballade** (buh-LOD) is a musical composition (or sometimes a poem) with a romantic quality.

- A **bight** is a U-shape (as in a rope); a **bite** is a bit of food; **byte** is a data-processing term.

- To **breach** is to break through, make a hole or gap in something. **Breech** means "the lower part of the human torso (often, the buttocks)." In a breech birth, the buttocks (or sometimes the feet) will come out first.

- To **broach** a subject is to bring it up for discussion; a **brooch** (pronounced the same, rhymes with **roach**) is a piece of jewelry.

- **Catalpa** is the name of a tree. **Catawbas** are American Indians living in South Carolina.

- **Chili** is a food; **Chile** is a country; **chilly** means cold.

- A **cymbal** is a percussion instrument—a brass disk that makes a clashing sound. A **symbol** is something (such as a statue or sign) that stands for something else.

- A **clue** is a hint, a bit of useful information. A **clew** is a corner of a sail.

- A **colonel** is a military officer. A **kernel** is the edible part of a nut (or the core of something).

- A **confidant** (or **confidante**, if it's a woman) is someone you confide in or tell your secrets to. You're **confident** when you're feeling good about your prospects.

- To **demur** is to object to something, to decline an opportunity or invitation (they invited her to run for office, but she demurred). **Demure** means modest and reserved in behavior.

- A **desert** is a dry, barren place—and for most of us, one **desert** is plenty. On the other hand, we might want a second sweet treat, or **dessert**. If you get your "just deserts" (pronounced like **desserts**), you're getting what you deserve.

- A **dinghy** (ding-ee) is a small boat; **dingy** (din-jee) means dim, dull, dirty.

- A **discreet** person is careful, especially in keeping secrets. **Discrete** means separate, distinct. Notice that in **discreet** the **e**'s are together, like two discreet people whispering secrets, and that in **discrete** they are separate.

- A **doe** is a deer, a female deer. **Dough** is a mix of flour and liquid (or slangily, money).

- We work to **earn** money. An **erne** (sometimes spelled **ern**) is a sea eagle. An **urn** is a large vase.

- A **gait** is a way of walking or running; a **gate** is a door in a fence.

- A **callus** is a thickening of the skin, often on the foot. **Callous** means insensitive to the feelings of others. So we could say one means hardness of the sole, the other means hardness of the soul.

- When **lead** rhymes with **bed**, it's a noun or adjective, as in "made of lead" or "lead pencil." But the present-tense verb **lead** rhymes with **bead** and its past tense is spelled **led**. "You led yesterday, so he will lead today—if he'll get the lead out of his feet."

- A **magnet** is something (usually metal) that attracts other things (also usually metal). A **magnate** is a person of great influence and importance and usually of great wealth.

- A **manor** is the main house of an estate or plantation. **Manner** means "method or style."

- **Martial** (from Mars, god of war) means warlike, or related to the military. A **marshal** is an officer (of the military, a court, a parade, etc.). And the **Marshall** Islands are named for Captain John **Marshall**.

- A **moose** is a large hoofed animal. The term **mousse** refers to either a dessert (such as chocolate mousse) or to foamy stuff used to hold hair in place.

- **Noble** (NO-b'l) means "admirable, excellent, of high quality." The **Nobel** (no-BELL) is a prize for outstanding achievement, named for Alfred Nobel.

- **Ordnance** is military weaponry and ammunition. An **ordinance** is a local law or regulation.

- Remember that **palate** helped you taste what you ate. **Palette** holds an artist's paints and thus is a little friend, a "pal-ette." And you **let** a **pal** help you move stuff on that **pallet**.

- A **peek** is a quick look (think of the two "e's" as two eyes). A **peak** is a top (as in mountain peak). And **pique** means to arouse feelings—often irritation, resentment or curiosity. (The feeling itself can be called **pique**.)

- A **phase** (pronounced **faze**) is a stage in a process. To **faze** is to "disturb, disconcert"—often used in the negative, as "The problems did not faze her at all."

- The noun is **prophecy** (PROF uh see); the verb is **prophesy** (PROF uh sigh).

- To **reek** is to give off a strong (often unpleasant) smell. To **wreak** is to make something happen—usually something unpleasant, as in "The market crash wreaked havoc with my retirement funds."

- Words **rhyme** when they have similar-sounding endings. **Rime** (also called hoarfrost) is a thin coating of ice, as on grass or trees.

- As a verb, to **rifle** means to ransack, to search without permission; to **riffle** means to flip through pages and is often used with **through**: If thieves **rifle** my chest of drawers, I hope they don't **riffle** through my diary.

- A **role** is always a noun, either a part in a play or any such specific assignment. **Roll** can be a chunk of bread or the tat-a-tat of a drum. It is also frequently a verb: "When the gang's all here, your **role** is to **roll** out the barrel."

- A **route** is a road or passageway. A **root** is the underground part of a plant. To **rout** is to defeat and send scurrying away in disorder.

- **Sheik**, a noun for a male Arab leader, fits the "e before i/ It's as easy as pie" rule. And don't confuse it with **chic**, the sound-alike adjective for "fashionable."

- There's a reliable memory hook for **stationary** and **stationery**. The one with the "a" before the "r" means "staying **at** the same place, not moving" while the word with the "e" refers to l**e**tt**e**r paper.

- **Straight** or **strait**? The second spelling means narrow, as in the narrow passage of water called a **strait**. And when Houdini escaped from a narrow restraining jacket, it was a **strait**jacket.

- **Urban** refers to a city, while **urbane** describes a person whose manner is elegant and sophisticated.

- It's **vane** as in weather vane, **vain** as in inappropriately proud of yourself, and **vein** as in the bodily companion to artery.

- A **veil** can be a literal piece of cloth like a bridal **veil**, or a figurative **veil** of silence. Don't confuse either with **vale**, similar to **valley** and **dale**.

- Don't confuse **viola** (the musical instrument) with **voila** (vwaLA), the French import meaning "Look!" or "There it is!"

- **Waive** means "to give up a right," while **wave** is to make the hand gesture of greeting or farewell.

- The word **wench** is archaic or jocular for a woman, and is very different from **winch**, a cranking or hauling mechanism.

- A **yen** is a longing, but **yin** exists to be partnered with **yang** as the embodiment of contrasting forces.

TAKE A (SPELLING) TIP

Unfortunately, most so-called rules about English spelling can take you only so far. So take a look at the following tips and start thinking about those execeptions.

- **Dyeing** (changing color) is an exception to the rule "Drop a final 'e' before adding 'ing.'" Other exceptions include **shoeing**, **hoeing**, and **fleeing**.

- When spelling **minuscule**, think "minus," not "mini." If you subtract material, you make something smaller, or even **minuscule**.

- This often **misspelled** word is a classic example of the prefix "mis-" followed by a word starting with an "s." That's why there's a double "s."

- The "k" in the middle of **picnicking** helps retain the pronunciation.

- **Sieve** is an example of the much-quoted "i-before-e" rule.

- **Shoeing** has three vowels in a row. This is one of those exceptions to the rule about dropping the vowel before "-ing."

- You might see the variant **spacial**, but **spatial** is much more common for the adjective referring to space.

- **Truly** drops an e before the -ly while **sincerely** keeps it.

- A ruler of old Russia is most commonly spelled **czar**, and can also be spelled **tsar** or even **csar**, but **czar** is more common in American use and is the form almost always used informally to mean "someone in charge," as in "grammar czar" or "budget czar."

- Technically, **whiskey** is the proper spelling only for Irish whiskey (as opposed to the **whisky** from Scotland or other countries), but in the United States it's customarily used for all of them.

About the Authors

David Hatcher (Winston-Salem, NC) has taught communication skills for three universities and more than twenty government and private-industry clients. He has written and cowritten several books, workbooks, and other training materials on writing, vocabulary, proofreading, editing, and related subjects. Mr. Hatcher earned an MA from Indiana University. His writing has been published in the *Washington Post*, national magazines, and a collection of short stories by Mid-Atlantic writers.

Jane Mallison (New York, NY) has taught on the middle school, high school, and college levels. She currently teaches at Trinity School in New York, where she was head of the English Department for more than twenty years. She has worked extensively with the writing section of the SAT tests and continues to work with the Advanced Placement English examination. She has an MA from Duke University, and is the author of several books on vocabulary development, grammar, and reading for pleasure. She was the runner-up in her junior high spelling bee, done in by the word "souvenir."